PRE-SCHOOL — PLAY — ACTIVITIES

PRE-SCHOOL
— PLAY —
ACTIVITIES

Edwina Conner

Macdonald

Conceived and produced by
Swallow Publishing Ltd
Swallow House
11-21 Northdown Street
London N1 9BN

Editor: Anne Yelland
Editorial consultant: Philippa Stratton
Art director: David Allen
Designer: Su Martin
Photography: John Campbell
Illustrator: Nadine Wickenden
Picture research: Catherine Tilley
Studio: Del and Co

First published in Great Britain in
1987 by Macdonald & Co
(Publishers) Ltd
Greater London House
Hampstead Road
London NW1 7QX

Members of BPCC plc

British Library Cataloguing in Publication Data

Conner, Edwina
Pre-School Play Activities
1. Educational games
I. Title
155.4'22   BF721

ISBN 0-356-11803-7
ISBN 0-356-11804-5 Pbk

Typeset by Typecast, London N16
Printed and bound in Spain by Mateu Cromo

Contents

Foreword 7
Introduction 8
Your store cupboard of materials 10

Indoor activities
Drawing and painting 12
More about painting 14
Printing 16
Clever collages 18
Telling the time 20
Fantasy games 22
Making puppets 24
Toys and mobiles 26
Sorting and collecting 28
Understanding numbers 30
Weighing and measuring 32
Memory games 34
How things work 36
Experiments in science 38
Modelling 40
Playing shop 42
Sewing, weaving and threading 44
Making music 46
Look after your body 48
Get knitting! 50
Jigsaw puzzles 52
Loving books 54
Learning to read 56
Keeping pets 58

Outdoor activities
Garden adventures 60
Outdoor games 62
It's raining! 64
Windy days 66
Animal tracks and trails 68
Out and about 70
All about trees 72
Trips out 74

Seasonal activities
At the pond 76
How things grow 78
Visiting a farm 80
Plants from scraps 82
Off for a picnic 84
Wild flowers 86
Fun with water 88
At the beach 90
Playing with sand 92
Keeping insects and garden animals 94
Snow and ice 96
Birds and birdwatching 98

Special occasions
At the theatre 100
Throwing a party 102
Mother's Day 104
Hallowe'en 106
Spring festivals 108
Winter festivals 110
Festival cooking 114

Book list 116
Useful addresses 117
Acknowledgements 118
Index 119

In the field of child care there are a great many books on the shelves which deal with spots and tummy upsets, nappy rash and feeding problems in which as parents we seek guidance and reassurance when our babies and toddlers show signs of distress and we are in need of greater experience.

As the child grows and develops the needs change and now we need assistance and reassurance to enable us as parents to give our children the best start they can have in life. Psychologists suggest that half a child's intellectual growth takes place in the years 0-4 and   most by the time he or she is eight. An awesome responsibility which is put into perspective when we realize that children learn and develop through play. By exploring, experimenting, investigating, questioning and doing, children build their knowledge of the world around them and learn to think and reason.

At the present time there is a great deal of pressure from all sides to start children in formal education at an early stage but if they have not had the time to play and explore their world they are going to find this experience difficult. Just as building a jigsaw puzzle is much harder if you do not start with the edges, so must it be for children to build a complete picture if they are given new experiences and challenges before they have had time to experiment, explore and investigate the immediate world around them.

Here is a book of practical and simple ideas which you can share with your child as this learning goes on. Though at times it is exhausting to have an 'under five' around, it is the most rewarding relationship and experience if you can enjoy being and doing together during the day at the times when there is no pressure on either of you. The child's confidence and self-esteem are increased as you talk together about the way the paint runs, the dough moulds, the pictures in a book, the way the seeds grow and the wind blows the leaves from the tree. Through this looking, doing, feeling and expressing the jigsaw edge will take shape and the child have a picture of the world that grows in clarity as the pieces fit together.

Jennie Shaw
Pre-School Playgroups Association

Introduction

The years before a child goes to school can never be recaptured. This is the time when so much is discovered and absorbed. Every day there is something new to wonder at, think about, observe and create. It is a very exciting and joyful time for children and parents alike.

But even if you are the most inventive parent you will sometimes face the thought, 'What do I do now?', especially if the child is your first. Your child has ceased to be a baby, and is a lively, mobile, curious and highly individual person. You no longer have the support of doctors, midwives or health visitors, but your child is a long way off going to school. Even if he or she goes to a nursery, day-care centre or playgroup, there is still the rest of the day and the weekends, when it's you, the parents, who are on call.

As every first-time parent finds out, you do not have to 'do' that much; given the right things to play with, children will often entertain themselves. But there are times when you will want to or have to involve yourself more, and children will always benefit from your time and enjoyment of the activities. Even if you are busy doing something else, a little thought put into their play will make it more valuable than simply giving them some paints and letting them get on with it.

Young children learn through play, not through formal teaching, and what may strike you as an essentially pointless activity is, in fact, the best way for a child to explore the world and to find out about his or her own capabilities. That does not mean that anything goes – there are a few guidelines which should help when you come to organize an activity.

First of all, pick a time when all of you have some energy and enthusiasm and not when you or the children are exhausted or hungry. After a busy morning at playgroup or nursery school they will not want to concentrate on something like a word game – certainly not until they've had a meal and a quiet time with a picture book.

Secondly, a play session with you should be relaxing. Never try to force children to concentrate. You can suggest and cajole a little, but if you sense a lack of interest, find something they want to do and let them get on with it; try the activity again later or the next day.

Don't make too much fuss about mess. Children will not be able to relax or become really absorbed in something if they (or you) are constantly worried about the odd spillage or paint splodge on their clothes. Having special clothes for messy activities is an answer.

8

Finally, tempting though it is, do not take over an activity. You will learn a good deal by observing how the children explore their materials and use them in quite different ways from those you had suggested or expected. That's how they find things out for themselves.

Using this book

Although this book is intended for two-to-fives, with the enormous changes that age span encompasses, I have not indicated an age for each activity, because I found it extremely difficult to decide how to do that. I know from experience that whereas one two-year-old will happily paint for hours alone, another will refuse to sit still for a moment. Often it is not a question of age but of motivation, personality and the ability to concentrate. Each child is quite different. For the same reason, the activities are not graded according to levels of difficulty. Each can easily be adapted to suit the needs and likes of your own family or group.

The activities are organized into different sections – indoor, outdoor, seasonal and special occasions – so that there should be something for every child at all times of the year.

Although the book is mainly addressed to parents, it has been written with playgroups and other care centres in mind. Many of the activities are suitable for groups, and all can be done with other children around, even if they are engaged in other pastimes.

Playgroups, nursery schools, and day-care centres

The main value of a playgroup (or nursery school or day-care centre) is that it offers children a chance to play with others of their own age. This means that they have to share their toys, get used to being separated from their family for a period, to begin to control their own feelings and take the feelings of others into account. They also become familiar with other adults, which is good practice for coping with the teachers they will meet at school later on.

Playgroups in Great Britain are usually run informally, with other mothers present. The best have a happy atmosphere and are an extension of a child's home. Playgroups belonging to the Pre-School Playgroups Association receive advice, support and training from them.

The only way to find a playgroup, nursery or day-care centre for your children is to ask around the neighbourhood and go along with your child for at least a session. Note the atmosphere, the relationship between the adults and the children and the range of activities on offer.

If you don't like the playgroup or day-care centre or nursery school you don't have to send your children to it. You have two other choices. Set up your own (see addresses on page 117) or keep the children at home, making sure they have plenty of young visitors to play with.

Finally, although the activities in this book are educational, don't treat them too seriously. Everything a child does is in some way educational, and the main aim of this book is to suggest ways to channel a child's natural inquisitiveness and curiosity. The important thing about play is that it is fun, and if an activity ceases to be so the child will stop it. The fun is there for the adults too – the excitement and joy are there to be shared.

Your store cupboard of materials

Anyone with young children soon gets to know instinctively what to keep for creative activities. It's a good idea to keep a cupboard (or part of one) especially for this purpose or you'll find piles of eggboxes and scraps of material all over the house, making it look like the home of an eccentric collector.

If you use labelled shoeboxes, piled on top of each other, for different bits of equipment, you will be able to move unerringly to the right place at the right time. Unless you can lay your hands on the materials you or your child wants straight away, you'll waste precious play session time searching round the house for them, and by the time they come to light, everybody's enthusiasm will have waned, there will be frustration all round and time will be up.

Useful rubbish

Scrap paper and cardboard Old magazines, newspapers, greetings cards, shelf-lining paper, greaseproof paper and paper bags, paper doilies, tissue paper, patterned and plain wallpaper, straws, postcards, index cards, mail shots, circulars (for papier mâché), computer printout, rolls of newsprint.

Corrugated cardboard, tubes from paper towels and toilet rolls, matchboxes, cereal and other food boxes, large cardboard boxes.

Fabric Velvet, hessian (burlap), felt, old sheets, fur fabric, cotton, bias binding and other edging, clean disposable cleaning cloths – anything patterned or plain.

Pots and boxes Ice-cream cartons, yoghurt, cottage cheese and cream pots, cheese boxes, foil containers, cake cases, plastic cups, take-away food boxes, margarine tubs, shoeboxes, herb boxes, glass jars.

Collage and modelling materials Shoelaces, pipe cleaners, yarns, beads, buttons, sequins, ice-lolly (popsicle) sticks, toothpicks, glitter, foil (such as yoghurt carton and milk-bottle tops), used matchsticks, home-made paste (see page 18).

What to buy

Drawing materials Coloured chalks, thin and thick wax crayons, fat pieces of charcoal, felt tips and soft pencils are all useful. White, coloured and black paper, loose or in pads, is widely available.

Clay and dough There is a recipe for a versatile playdough on page 40. Ordinary modelling clay or special clay that does not have to be oven-baked can be bought at a craft supplier.

Paint Powder paint is the most economical for young children, though poster paint is also available in large plastic bottles and can be decanted into smaller containers. Older children might like to experiment with watercolours, though these need much more care.

Brushes Buy some ordinary thick brushes made for children, but let them try out pastry brushes, new household paintbrushes, old toothbrushes and some thinner, watercolour brushes too.

Brushes need to be washed in soapy water after use and stored carefully so that they don't bend or 'fray' out at the end.

Miscellaneous

Jigsaw puzzles, books, toy money, soft toys and dolls, musical instruments, microscope, magnifying glass, magnets, fishing-net, dressing-up clothes.

Drawing and painting

Messing about with crayons and pencils is usually the earliest creative activity young children enjoy. Because they are so personal, involving concentration and individual ideas, and are expressions of all kinds of inner thoughts and worries, drawing and painting are important ways for children to show you what they feel about themselves and their place in the world.

The first stage involves grasping a fat crayon and dashing it backwards and forwards across a piece of paper, or on the wall! And a very satisfying and delightful business it is to be able to make your mark, inspect the quality of the colour as you press harder or softer and listen to the squeak of crayon on paper.

As a child gains more muscle control, these first scribbles will become more considered; lines will start and finish and go in a particular direction, first up and down and side to side and later in circles. Sometimes these scribbles will represent pictures. What looks like a meaningless mess of lines and circles will be entitled 'Daddy in the garden' or 'My dog, Spot'. At other times your child will simply be experimenting with colour and design. Encouraging remarks about the masterpieces will always be appreciated.

Providing drawing materials

The development of scribble into lines and then to recognizable drawings is a universal process which all children seem to go through, whatever their background, nationality or culture. They don't need to be taught how to do this: it happens automatically as their powers of observation and control over their muscles develop.

All you need to do is to provide plenty of good fat crayons and coloured chalks, and white, coloured and black paper. Since walls are so tempting, try a making a bedroom blackboard, and supplying a box of chalk (see pages 56-7). That way the children can pick up the chalk whenever they feel like it, and you'll save yourself having to set out and clear away drawing materials every day.

Painting

Painting has even more appeal for children than drawing. It is a bolder activity, giving a feeling of immense power. They can make a picture, destroy it, or change it, with just one or two brave sweeps of the brush.

Safety notes
Paints no longer contain lead, but that does not mean they are quite harmless. A child who swallows a glass of mixed powder paint is likely to be very sick. When using long brushes or other long objects, watch out that they do not get used as weapons.

Attacking a piece of paper with crayons and experimenting with a good wash of colour are all part and parcel of the creative process.

Colours can be sloshed on, mixed and swirled for interesting effects. It is a thoroughly absorbing activity and there are few children who do not find it irresistible.

Splodges and patches of bright colour are characteristic of children's first paintings. At first the 'pattern' will be haphazard, but gradually they will choose their colours according to preference, and begin to make considered choices about where the blobs of colour should go.

One day a real picture will emerge, with no help from you. Most children have an inbuilt ability and desire to create a pattern and shape with paint, but don't tell them to draw or paint a particular scene or object, as they could be put off if they are dissatisfied with the results.

Paint and paper

It is important for children to be able to paint whenever they want to and with the minimum amount of fuss or trouble. A roll of lining paper or newsprint which you can spread over the kitchen table or on a groundsheet on the floor is useful, as are ready-mixed powder paints in pluggable containers for easy storage. Thick brushes are the most popular, but supply some thinner ones and also some household paint-brushes for covering big areas. New ones are best, just in case old ones have been used with paints containing lead, paint-stripper, or other toxic materials. An easel, or a stack of paper that can be attached to the wall and torn off once used, is also popular and quickly available. Make sure the children are wearing aprons – but all the same be prepared for some paint to go under them on to clothes – supply dust sheets or newspapers and let them get on with it.

More about painting

An early interest in painting should mean your children keep a creative ability throughout their school years. If they come to it later they may well be too inhibited to experiment and make mistakes. So go on encouraging children to paint when they feel like it. There are plenty of interesting activities that can be introduced to make use of the various and glorious properties of paint.

Let your children try out all kinds of equipment. Sponges make very satisfactory patterns.

All kinds of materials

Brushes aren't the only tools for painting. Bits of sponge, straws, toothbrushes, and kitchen roll all create interesting effects. Blowing a dollop of paint through a straw will send the paint off in odd directions on the paper, and 'spraying' paint from the end of a toothbrush will give an effect the Impressionists would have been proud of. Masses of newspaper, waterproof sheets and old clothes will minimize the mess, and you can always move outdoors if the weather is good.

Finger painting

This is full of potential for 'self-expression'! Mix some flour with powder paint and water so that you have a thick coloured paste. Spread this on a tray so that the children can put their whole hand in if they like, squish it around and squeeze it through their fingers. They may never get any further than this, but if they want to, show them how to paint with their fingers, make hand-prints and thumb blobs in different directions on a big sheet of paper, or even better, a laminated table top.

Stencils

Cut simple shapes (stars, triangles, animals) out of thick card, lay the card on paper and then let the children paint over it. Paper doilies make interesting stencils, though they have to be kept still for satisfactory results. Also try folding a plain piece of paper and cut out any shapes that occur to you to make your own stencils.

Computer paper, with its perforated edges, can be used to create dotted borders.

Wax and paint

There are several ways of using wax to create pictures. Show the children how to draw a simple pattern on a piece of paper with the blunt end of a white candle, then apply a thick layer of paint. See what happens. Or get them to cover a sheet of strong paper with patches or stripes of brightly coloured wax crayons and then obliterate the pattern yourself with a black crayon. They then carefully scratch the black away, and a new picture emerges.

With your supervision, the children can also melt the end of a wax crayon over a candle (remove the paper first) and then quickly draw the crayon over paper. The texture of the wax is quite different when it has melted – smooth, thick and shiny.

Mixing colours

Children nearly always go for the bright, primary colours when they are painting, so it's a good opportunity to explain that from red, blue and yellow we can make any colour we want.

They will love experimenting, though to start with most of their efforts will turn out dark, murky brown or almost black, which might be discouraging. Keeping their brushes clean and providing plenty of fresh water will help keep the colour pure. You can point out how different quantities of one colour can lighten or darken the effect, and show them how a few drops of water can alter a colour.

Blowing a sea monster into shape.

15

Printing

There's something very satisfying about thumping an object down on a piece of paper and making a mark – again and again and again! Children seem to take to printing with little encouragement. All you have to do is provide paper, rich coloured paint and things to print with. Cotton reels, wood blocks, corks, leaves and twigs, sponges, string, clothes pegs (pins), keys, and buttons all take on a more interesting dimension pressed into paint and on to paper.

You don't have to do much in these early stages but watch as it may stop children experimenting for themselves if you try to get them to produce perfect works of art. Some of the ideas here will need your guidance, but even then give the children as much freedom as possible. *Note:* Add a little paste and a squeeze of detergent to the paint. The paste thickens and the detergent helps to get spilt paint off clothes and skin.

The paint pad
Put an old but clean sponge in a paint tray and pour the paint over it. Objects can then be pressed on to the sponge. This is easier than using the paint in the tray.

Hand- and footprints
These are very satisfying and good fun, particularly footprints. Use a long piece of lining paper or newsprint and lay it on newspaper. Put the paint tray and pad at one end. The first child dips his or her feet in paint (your steadying hand is needed here) and walks slowly across the paper, turning this way and that. A refill may be needed halfway down the line. When one lot of footprints is dry, another child, using a second colour, can follow. The different sized and shaped feet, weaving in and out of each other, make a super design. Grown-up feet and hands add to the picture!

Hand- and fingerprints can be used together to make an interesting pattern.

Roller printing
Use an ordinary paint roller, or the cardboard tube from a kitchen or toilet roll. Wrap string or wool around this, then roll it in the paint and across the paper. Leaves and lace can be roller-printed too.

LETTER PRINTING
Using corks and a sharp knife, cut out letters (lower case), remembering that they should be back to front, for the children to print with. Children are often very interested in letters and this will help them recognize them, but don't turn the activity into a reading lesson unless they *ask* how to print a particular word!

BLOCK PRINTING
Older children might enjoy this. To make repeat patterns with more fiddly flat or delicate materials, use a block. Glue on leaves, pieces of string, or wallpaper with a definite raised pattern. The block can then be dipped in the paint and printed.

Marbling
Older children might enjoy this even messier activity which produces very attractive results. Pour some water into a bowl or baking tray and add some artists' oil paints or leftover household gloss paint (but note that this sticks to skin). Swirl this about with a stick and get your small printers to float a piece of paper on the surface for about 30 seconds before removing it and lying it flat on newspaper to dry. The results with a bit of luck will look rather like the endpapers of some 19th-century books.

Wrapping paper
White or coloured tissue paper or unwaxed shelf-lining paper make good bases for home-printed giftwrap with the individual touch.

Wax prints
Give the children a candle each. They draw with this on a piece of paper, haphazardly or with a design in mind (it doesn't matter), then dip the paper in the paint tray (remove the paint pad) and let the picture dry flat. The paint will not stick to the wax.

Messy but glorious hand- and footprints lend a new look to a length of lining paper.

17

Clever collages

If you've been wondering why you've been collecting all those eggboxes, bits of string, ribbon, buttons, beads, leaves and foil bottle and carton tops, now's the time to put them all to good use. Give the children some paste (see below), a few of these items and a good sized piece of paper each and they will let rip. They will enjoy playing about with different materials and textures – discovering what is soft, what hard, what bends or curves and what breaks. Talk with them too about pattern and colour mixing. They'll get paste everywhere to start with and no doubt make every attempt to stick themselves to the paper, but with practice will find a reasonably efficient way of attaching collage to background.

Paper collage

Stop throwing away all those paper bags, gift wrapping paper, chocolate paper (candy bar wrappers), wallpaper ends, doilies and other dustbin fodder; they are now officially artists' materials! Choose all sorts of paper – smooth and shiny, coloured, patterned, and so on. A few snips of the scissors will produce plenty of interesting shapes and textures for sorting and sticking.

Mosaics add a 'jigsaw' dimension to paper collage. Metal patchwork templates are best, but cardboard will do. Use them to cut out geometric paper shapes and let the children fit them together into a design.

Paper sculpture collage is a bit more fiddly but worth the effort. Folded into concertina shapes, made into spirals, little balls or tubes or curled round a pencil, that flat piece of paper becomes a staircase, a pile of logs or a football. These three-dimensional objects can be painted and incorporated in a two-dimensional picture.

Fabric collage

All types of fabric can be stuck on to paper or felt to make lovely patterns with various textures. Co-opt buttons, sequins and lace and hunt out colourful bits of wool and embroidery silks. If you think your children will really enjoy this activity, ask them to draw good-sized pictures of each member of the family and find appropriate material to 'dress' up everybody. For added realism, the clothes can be 'accessorized' with lace cuffs and collars, buttons for dresses, zips for trousers, ties, hats, ribbons, and bows, so keep these items too.

Safety notes
Use round-ended scissors and keep a watchful eye on them. Make sure that buttons, sequins and other small objects that might get swallowed are kept away from the two-year-olds.

MAKING YOUR OWN COLLAGE PASTE
You'll need:
100 g (4 oz./1 cup) flour
1 tablespoon salt
cold water to mix

1 Mix the flour, water and salt in a small saucepan with enough water to make a creamy paste.
2 Bring the mixture to the boil and simmer for five minutes.

The paste will keep in a jam-jar (jelly glass) with a lid in the fridge for several days and can be used for other craft activities.

Nature

Bring a little bit of outdoors inside. Leaves, bits of bark, seeds, catkins, rose petals, dried flowers, and so on can be stuck on to a piece of wood to make an unusual, seasonal picture.

Rubbings

This is an absorbing activity, helpful for those all-too-frequent 'I don't know what to do' times. Suggest that the children take some coloured paper round the house and look for textured objects to 'rub'. Vinyl tiles, coins, left-over pieces of embossed wallpaper or cork tiles, and raffia mats are all good to rub. The rubbings can then be combined to make a collage.

Once you've started them off, children will soon come up with collage ideas of their own and from time to time their enthusiasm will drive them to produce something that you, at least, consider worthy of a modern art gallery.

Almost anything can be used to make a collage. Encourage the children to work out which is the best material for a particular job.

19

Telling the time

Children find time a very difficult concept. Connecting a particular time to a regular activity helps get the notion across.

Even in these days of digital time-keeping, learning to read a clock face is an important skill. But it's by no means easy. Time has little meaning for small children, because they do not take responsibility for getting themselves up, going to playgroup, fixing meals and going to bed – you do it all for them.

Nor do they have much understanding of the terms 'last week', 'in a few days' time' or 'the day before yesterday'. Even the days of the week are difficult to distinguish. To them there is only what has gone, what is happening now and what will be happening next. In particular, try explaining the concept of 'tomorrow' to a three-year-old – the next day he or she is likely to ask 'Is it tomorrow now?'!

So learning to tell the time involves various complicated concepts which should not be underestimated. In addition, of course, children have to be able to recognize numbers up to 12, understand halves and quarters, how the space between 12 and 1 can represent five minutes, and why, when the big hand is pointing to the figure 8, it is actually *20* minutes to the hour. The whole business can take several months to master. It's unlikely that you can even make a start with a child under four and then it's best to go very slowly. When they can do it, you'll all be justifiably proud.

The clock face

Buy a clock face with hands, or make one from a piece of strong card, and fix the hands at the centre with a split pin metal fastener. Attach this to a larger, square piece of card that can be propped up on a table against the wall. Next to getting-up time, breakfast time, playgroup or nursery school time, and meal times, draw pictures to represent the activity.

Write '7 (or whenever) o'clock is bedtime', '5 o'clock is suppertime' on separate pieces of card which can be propped up at the bottom of the clock card. Change the hands and the cards every day, until the children can answer the questions, 'What time do you get up?', 'What time do we set off for playgroup?' and so on. They'll soon learn to move the hands to the right position to correspond with the words on the card or the answer to the question.

Shade the four quarters of the clock face with different colours so that the children begin to understand these ideas. The times in between should probably be saved until they start school.

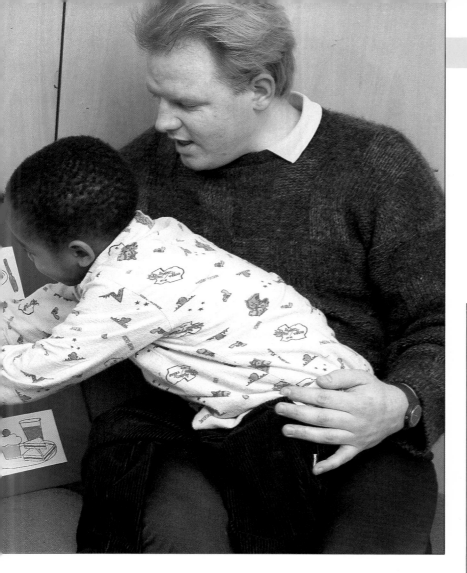

Time passing

Young children will be pretty interested in this fascinating idea of passing time that adults seem to be so worried about, and will respond if you make a conscious effort to talk to them about the morning, afternoon, evening, early, late, yesterday, tomorrow, the day after tomorrow, next week.

'We always go to playgroup in the morning, and have supper in the evening. When it's night time we go to bed.'

'We've been waiting for the bus for five minutes. Let's see how much longer we have to wait...five minutes more.' Point to your watch.

'Tomorrow we will go to the shops, and the day after tomorrow we'll go to the park.'

Days and months

Buy or make a picture calendar showing a month at a time. Draw on it familiar activities – the weekly swim or visit to Grandma – and special trips that you've been on and that are planned. Talk about it. 'So we've got to wait four days until we go to the zoo, but we can see Granny on Tuesday; that's in two days' time.'

THE SEASONS

Register spring, summer, autumn and winter with a picture or collage and a list of words or a poem to describe each.

The North Wind Doth Blow
The north wind doth blow,
And we shall have snow,
And what will the robin do then,
    poor thing?
He'll sit in a barn,
And keep himself warm
And hide his head under his
    wing, poor thing!

Anon.

Spring
A bluetit sat on my windowsill,
'It's Spring,' he said, 'trill, trill, trill
Look out of your window,
What can you see?
One crocus, two snowdrops, and
    buds on the trees.'

'Oh good,' I said, 'Spring is here
The ice has melted, the snow
    disappeared,
Everything looks so green and
    new
And you look so pretty, dear
    bluetit, too.'

Fantasy games

Playing house is very often the first fantasy game children enjoy. It soon becomes clear, even to a two-year-old, that grown-ups run the home and organize the cooking, cleaning, childcare and shopping. For four or five years their home is the world in microcosm. Joy, anger, love, and sadness are all part of this world, and the relationships between all members of the family are the main ones they know.

So a playhouse with dressing-up clothes and other props helps children act out roles together, explore that world, and provide the opportunity to be grown up for an hour or two.

The house

Very often rugs, sticks and pieces of furniture skilfully juxtaposed provide a perfect temporary house with dark places to hide away from grown-ups. A more permanent home for two small children can be made from two giant cardboard boxes (washing-machine size) cut open and stuck together. Use a sharp craft knife to cut windows and a door, then paint the roof, stick on a chimney, and paint creepers up the side of the house.

Provide a few pots and pans for cooking games, a doll's tea set, some books, colouring materials, dolls and soft toys, a doll's pram (carriage) and bedclothes and the children will play happily for hours.

A 'garden' can be made from a sheet of chipboard or hardboard painted green with a path winding up it and some flowers dotted about, or a piece of flowery material will do. Provide toy watering cans and other garden tools.

Story-acting

Ask the children to dress up as two different characters. Unless they specifically ask for your ideas, let them choose who they want to be.

Then talk about a storyline together. So if one character is an ill little boy and the other is a doctor, discuss what will be wrong with the boy and ask what will happen when he is taken to the doctor. Of course you may end up with an engine driver and a circus performer, which will present *you* with a challenge too! Let them act out the play on their own, prompting them with the story if they dry up.

A slightly different version of this is to tell a short story of your own invention that involves plenty of characterization and adverbs. As you tell the story, ask the children to act it out at the same time. The children will probably want to add to the story or change it, so let them. This is a good game for increasing vocabulary too.

Dressing-up games

Keep handy a box of old clothes of all sorts, some pretty lace, ribbons, gold braid, a cloak, a cane, old umbrellas, gloves, socks, stockings and tights, belts, and hats of all kinds – anything unwanted and inherited from older members of the family.

Face paints, other old make-up (though check for allergic reactions) and perfume will also be welcomed. The characters that result from a free rummage among these clothes will provide the rest of the family with considerable entertainment.

Safety notes
Some children are allergic to adult make-up, so if you use this remove it straightaway if any such reaction appears.

Above: *Half office worker, half elegant lady. This little girl is making good use of the dressing-up box.*

Opposite: *Only clowns do the ironing? This is obviously an occasion demanding dress sense.*

23

Making puppets

Even the most makeshift puppets take on a lifelike quality and become 'friends' who sleep, cry, feel the heat or cold, get angry and generally behave just like people. Watch children play with a puppet and you'll learn a lot about their concerns and preoccupations, as they act out situations at home with members of the family and at playgroup or nursery school with good or difficult friends, or the playleader.

The puppets described here can all be made in a few minutes and do not need special skills.

Glove puppets

Glove puppets provide instant entertainment for a long journey or a wet afternoon. Pull a handkerchief over your hand, secure it with three rubber bands (elastics), over thumb, first and middle fingers, draw a face on your first finger with a black felt tip and presto – you have a ghostly presence! You'll need extra handkerchiefs for the children, of course, because they'll want to have a go too.

For slightly more elaborate puppets, gather together some fancy material, rubber bands, scraps of coloured paper, beads, feathers, felt tip pens, fabric paints and brushes, pipe cleaners and string. You can dress up your puppets with jewellery, hats made of paper, and hair made out of frayed string or cottonwool (absorbent cotton).

Alternatively, simply drape a piece of fabric over your hand, attach a face of beads and coloured paper, and use your first two fingers to make legs or fangs.

Sock puppets

Even simpler to make are strange sock creatures with long, flexible necks. Put a thumb in the heel and the rest of your fingers in the toe of a sock. Attach felt or paper ears, eyes and mouth and watch your puppet squirm. Sew a piece of red felt to the sole of the sock and it will become a mouth when you insert your thumb and fingers. It's quite extraordinary how these creatures spring to life in your hands.

Wooden spoon puppets

All you need for these are a set of wooden spoons of different sizes, rubber bands, paint, fabric to make clothes, cottonwool for hair, and pipe cleaners for arms (optional).

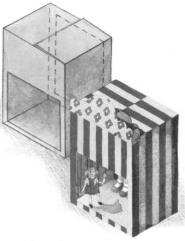

GLOVE PUPPET THEATRE

You'll need:
an extra large cardboard box (a washing-machine supplier should be able to let you have one)
some wallpaper or paint to decorate the box

1 Tape up the lid flaps, and cut out a hole in the bottom front of the box. Then cut out a large hole in the back big enough for the children to get in.
2 Decorate the outside with wallpaper, paint, paper mosaics or anything else the children fancy.
3 Turn the box upside-down and you have a glove puppet theatre with a roof. The children kneel inside.
4 If you have any string puppets, or can make these, you can turn the box the other way up with the hole at the bottom. The children stand behind holding the strings.
5 Fix a torch (flashlight) or a clip-on light on the inside of the theatre, turn off the living-room lights and watch the show.

A puppet show, run by adults, is great entertainment for children's parties, and will get plenty of audience participation.

These 'rod' puppets are very effective, and since wooden spoons come in so many shapes, a spoon 'family' wears a surprising variety of expressions.

If they prefer, the children can paint the bowl of the spoon with emulsion (flat) paint to provide a smooth surface for the features, but this is not really necessary. Use the back and front of each spoon, to give each character two expressions. Cut small holes in the fabric and push this on from the bottom, securing it at the neck with a rubber band. Wrap pipe cleaners round the stem of the spoon and let the fabric drape over these for the arms.

Sit the children behind a table, so they can hold the stems of the spoons above their heads. The audience watches from in front of the table. Alternatively, make a puppet theatre.

A few simple puppets and a home-made box theatre provide hours of entertainment for all concerned.

Toys and mobiles

Toys and decorations for children's rooms are notoriously expensive, and although the manufactured variety are attractive, children gain pleasure from making their own playthings or a gift for a friend or new-born baby. They'll be able to use all kinds of skills while keeping themselves happy and occupied.

Mobiles

Mobiles have a therapeutic quality. Watch a baby whose eye has been caught by a foil fish swinging in the wind or who is listening intently to the tinkling of a glass mobile – he or she will be totally absorbed and contemplative. An older child might like to make one for a new baby.

A simple mobile can be made from an ordinary wire coathanger. Use paper cut-outs, painted in bright colours, threaded through the top and tied to the coathanger, or shapes cut out of aluminium foil. These will twinkle and flash in the wind and sun. Two coathangers crossed over make a more complicated hanging mobile.

Toilet roll toys

The cardboard tubes from toilet rolls are an excellent base for all sorts of interesting toys.

Slippery Sid can be made from half a dozen cardboard toilet rolls. Show the children how to thread them on to a string to make a snake, then tape the ends of the string to the first and last roll. A sock stuffed with bits of material or old tights should be forced into the neck of the first roll. Stick on felt eyes and a nose, and paint his body green and brown. Slippery Sid can be pulled along with another piece of string attached to his neck.

An articulated doll requires eight to ten toilet rolls and three long pieces of string. Join two pieces of string together with a knot at the top and the middle, leaving the ends free for legs. Push two toilet rolls on to each leg and tape the string to the bottom rolls. Thread two toilet rolls on to the body and stick the ends of the string. Tie the third piece of string in the middle between the two body rolls and thread on arms – one or two more rolls for each. For the head, stuff the end of a sock with cottonwool (absorbent cotton) and push it down inside the first toilet roll. Make feet and arms in the same way.

Safety notes
Wire coathangers can be dangerous, and watch scissors and any other sharp objects. Metal foil needs watching too, as it can be sharp to little fingers.

Home-made toys are cheaper to make and have more play value and more personality than the shop variety.

Colour wheel

Using a pair of compasses, draw a circle on a piece of card, cut it out and draw on it two or three concentric circles. The children can fill in the circles carefully in different colours. Make two holes either side of the middle of the card and thread a piece of wool through, tying it so that the card stays in the middle of the wool. The children twist the wool tightly and let go sharply. The wheel will whizz round and round. What happens to the colours when the wheel is going round fast?

As an alternative to making circles on the card, the children might prefer to divide the piece of card into six or eight sections, and fill each in with a different colour. What does the wheel look like now when it whizzes round?

ALAN ALERT

This is a jumping doll that the children can help to make.

You'll need:
a stick about 40 cm
  (16 in.) long
beads
cottonwool
nylon tights
small cottage cheese
  carton or yoghurt pot
ribbon
glue
lengths of wool
cotton thread

1 Take the leg of a pair of tights and cut a length of 30 cm (12 in.). Tie one end of this with a piece of cotton and turn it inside-out so one end is open, one closed. Push some cottonwool into the closed end as a head and push in the end of the stick. Tie ribbon round the neck.
2 Make a round hole in the bottom of the carton and push the other end of the stick through the hole. Glue the open end of the stocking body round the top edge of the carton. Tie another ribbon round here or glue on a material edging.
3 Beads and felt make the features, and stick scraps of wool to Alan Alert's head to look like hair.
4 As the stick is pulled down, Alan disappears shyly into his house. Push it up and he pops up again full of confidence.

Sorting and collecting

Sorting and collecting come naturally to children. They'll need very little encouragement to hoard their treasures in corners, pile them up or lay them out, probably in a most inconvenient spot. Sequins, beads, buttons, badges, stickers, feathers, pebbles, fossils, shells, bits of string, ribbon and lace are all interesting collectables. As they sort them out – by colour, size, shape – they'll learn a lot about counting, weight and texture which will stand them in good stead when they start school.

Nuts can be sorted by colour, size or variety.

Let them have a go with the cutlery (keep sharp knives well out of the way), working out which section of the cutlery box each item should occupy. Children learn at different rates, of course, and while one may get the idea very quickly, another will simply fill each section in turn with spoons and forks regardless of shape or size. Let them have fun, trying to see their reflections in the back of a spoon (point out that it is upside-down because of the curve of the spoon), getting the sun to reflect off a shiny piece of cutlery on to your face or the wall, making a terrible clatter like an off-key steel band as they drop the cutlery (not your best!) into the tray. Experimenting in this way is all part of the learning process.

Buttons, beads, and dried peas can be sorted in the same way (use eggboxes or tins or larger boxes for storage). These items also make satisfactory, but different, noises, and all have their own special texture and feel.

Ask 'Which is smoother, a button or a pea?' Or drop different objects into a box. Can they tell from the sound which you are dropping when?

Once your children seem to have grasped the point of sorting, move on to make cards and draw, for example, two knives on one, three forks on another, four spoons on a third, together with large figures to represent the numbers. Put these cards in the boxes or cutlery divider and let them try to put the right number of implements in the right place.

Collectables can also be sorted according to colour (the children might like to assemble an 'orange corner' or a 'blue corner' in their bedroom for a while) and to size.

Beads and buttons make good colourful items to sort.

Making comparisons

If a child is collecting bird feathers, for instance, encourage him or her to talk to you about each comparatively. Is this feather bigger/smaller, shorter/longer, softer/harder/more prickly, paler/darker than that one? This is a good way to increase a child's vocabulary as well as getting him or her more interested in the activity.

Then move on to talk about your family. Is Daddy shorter/taller, fatter/thinner/more cuddly than Mummy/Mary/Grandpa? See if you can persuade them to lie down on a piece of paper (rolls of lining paper or newsprint are useful here) so that the children can draw round their bodies. They can fill in the faces and clothes afterwards and pin the 'models' on the walls.

Using collections

A good pile of lace, beads, string, ribbon or shells can be used for all kinds of creative activities. They can be made into collages to decorate the walls, or stuck on to special gift boxes. Beads and buttons can be threaded on to string or ribbon to make necklaces and bangles. This will involve more sorting according to size and colour to get a good effect.

You may end up with a house full of boxes, tins, plates, shoes, shelves and drawers of what you might be tempted to call rubbish, but remember that to your children it's a marvellous collection of 'interesting things'!

Safety notes
Small beads or buttons can be dangerous to young children, who like to put them in their mouths or use them to plug their noses and ears.

Understanding numbers

Sorting and collecting (see pages 28-9) are ideal activities for helping children make sense of numbers and for many this will be enough to take them through to the time they start school. Others will be ready to go further. These ideas for making sense of numbers include everyday activities and games you can play together.

Of course, children must never be forced to take part in games if they show no interest; this is only counter-productive. In the wrong circumstances these number games can cease to be fun for children so choose a time when you can relax yourself and give some attention to questions and difficulties.

Use big cards, no more than 20, for this pint-sized version of pelmanism.

What numbers mean

Although many children learn to count from one to ten quite early, they won't have much concept of what those words actually represent. So if you say, 'Bring me five potatoes' you may be presented with two or three or four. Probably all the child has grasped is that 'five' is more than 'one', but just how much more is not yet clear. Here are some ideas for helping them understand this more clearly, using things that are a normal part of their lives.

Matching numbers

Put two, three or four beads on the table and ask the children to match the number of beads with the same number of, say, building blocks or buttons, counting them out as they put them down.

Ask, 'Here are four buttons on my shirt. Are there enough buttonholes on this side to match them?' Or, 'I have four sandwiches here. Are there enough for everyone in the room?' Do not move on to larger numbers until they've grasped the smaller numbers.

Taking away and adding up

When a child takes a cake from a plate, say 'There were five cakes on that plate, now you've eaten one. How many are there left?' Or 'There are four cakes on this plate. If you put yours back again, how many will there be then?'

Number and picture cards

Draw six ladybirds or butterflies or little girls wearing spotted dresses on postcards. Each object is decorated with a number of spots from one to six. The children can arrange these in order from the lower number upwards or downwards. These cards can also be used for dominoes. The game is played as with ordinary dominoes – these cards just make it much more colourful!

Card pairs

Card pairs is an old-fashioned game, but excellent for helping children look for likenesses, and for improving concentration.

You can use ordinary playing cards, but the home-made variety are more fun. You'll need 20 postcards. On these draw five different objects, but matched in different ways. So if one of your objects is a cake, draw two cakes with one cherry on top, and two cakes with two cherries on top. If another is a button, two buttons could have two holes, and the other pair four holes, and so on.

To start with the children can just pair 'cakes' or 'buttons', then when they've got the idea they can match buttons with two holes, four holes, or one of each.

Alternatively, one pair of cakes could be pink, and another yellow, and these would have to be matched accordingly.

All you have to do is spread the cards out upside-down on the table or floor. Each player turns over two cards. If they match, according to the rules, they pick them up. If not, they are turned face down again and it is the next player's turn. Players have to remember where the cards are.

MAKING A WALLCHART

On a set of cards draw one teddy bear, two flowers, three ice-creams, four cakes, five biscuits (cookies), six buttons, and so on up to ten. The children will be happy to colour in the pictures. They can make a wallchart out of the cards, putting the objects in numerical order, and then sticking the chart on the bedroom or kitchen wall.

If they show an interest in drawing the figures representing these numbers, help them by tracing the outline of the figures in dots and letting them join them up. These can be added to the wallchart on the appropriate postcard.

Weighing and measuring

'Aren't you getting heavy?' beams a doting aunt, swinging your child in the air, and of course a quick check on the bathroom scales will show that she is absolutely right. Growing bigger and taller is a matter of great pride to children. Each time the scale pointer moves upwards and the mark on the door measuring their height creeps higher their self-esteem gets a boost. It's a small step from this personal interest in weighing and measuring to a more general understanding of the principles, so talk about them while you are playing together.

Which is heavier? Which lighter? Experiments at the kitchen table can include all kinds of household items.

Heavy and light

Choose a variety of objects, some the same size, some much bigger and others very small. Which are heavy and which light? Most children will assume that bigger objects are heavier than small ones. So just by looking at a large bag of hamster sawdust, for instance, it may be pronounced heavier than a hammer. Get them to pick them up and see for themselves.

If you have old-fashioned balancing scales or the toy variety, which can be bought quite cheaply, let them try balancing a small potato on one side and a bag of cornflakes on the other. They'll be surprised how much cereal they need to make the scales hover in the middle.

A picture chart showing the results of these experiments will make an attractive wallchart. For instance, one largish pebble could equal three carrots, or one carrot, one tomato and three boxes of matches. Use as many different objects as possible.

As children get older and get used to measuring out ingredients for cooking, they will become familiar with the numbers on the scales. Point out that weight is constant, that is 1 kg (2 lb.) of anything always weighs the same as 1 kg (2 lb.) of something else. Some children find this difficult to understand, but they can use the scales to experiment for themselves.

Measuring up

Once the children have grasped the idea of rulers and tape measures, there is no end to the objects that receive their attention. If you can get them to make comparisons of length or width, it will help their observation as well as skill in measuring and recognizing numbers.

Explain the difference between 'width' and 'length' and later on 'depth'. Ask, 'Which is wider – the chest of drawers or the table?', 'Which is longer – your nose or mine?' And, for older children, 'If this box is 8 cm (3 in.) long and that one is 10 cm (4 in.) long, how much longer is the second box?' This is practical maths and means much more to children than measuring lines on paper or doing abstract addition and subtraction sums.

Measuring irregular shapes

Straight-edged objects are easy to measure, but what about an amoeba-shaped pattern on a piece of paper, a round(ish) cake or a cat's tail? How can these be measured?

Don't just produce a piece of string (which is the answer!). See what your children suggest as a solution to the problem. They'll probably decide eventually that they can't use a ruler to wrap around a cake or a wiggly pattern, but need something flexible. The string can be laid alongside a ruler for accurate measuring afterwards.

Out and about

Who can jump further in the sandpit? Measuring with feet is just as valuable as using a tape measure. For children who can count, how many steps is it from your house to the bus-stop or other landmarks not too far from home?

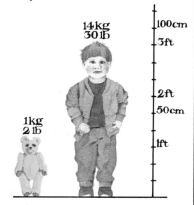

WEIGHING TEDDY
Teddies, dolls and other favourite toys can be weighed on the bathroom scales and measured on the wall. The children's weight and height set alongside teddy's on a wallchart will allow you to talk about how much less teddy weighs, how much smaller he is, and how the children are even bigger than teddy this year than they were last year.

14kg
30lb

100cm
3ft

2ft
50cm

1kg
2lb

1ft

Memory games

Babies start to memorize as soon as they open their eyes. The faces of adults close to them, the warm feelings of being rocked and cuddled, how to suckle milk, exchanging smiles with you – all these become longed-for activities. If these familiar sensations are withdrawn, the baby not surprisingly feels deprived.

Memory, then, comes naturally, but practice in the pre-school years helps children communicate more effectively and also to take some responsibility for their possessions and for some aspects of their own timetable. It's a great help too in learning to read, which involves (among other things) remembering the shape and pattern of letters, words and phrases.

Concentration time is short. Don't force children to play these games, and if they do show interest, play for only a short time. Children feel a failure if they are slow to remember something, so it's better not to introduce too much competition (in the shape of an older, more competent child for instance).

Card pairs (described on page 31) is also a useful matching/memory game.

The tray game
This is a good game for a small party of five-year-olds. Arrange ten or so different objects on a tray and let the children see them for about half a minute. Then cover the tray with a cloth and ask each child to whisper to you the objects he or she remembers. The one who gets most right is the winner.

'My grandmother went to market'
This is a real tester for adults as well as for children! It needs a considerable amount of concentration, but can be played with any number of people. Start, 'My grandmother went to market and she bought a bicycle (or whatever).' Player no. 2 continues, 'My grandmother went to market and she bought a bicycle and a fluffy chick.' The third player adds a third object, and so on, but each player must recite all the items grandmother has bought before adding another purchase. It doesn't matter what outlandish things she packs into her shopping basket. The early items are easier to remember, because they are repeated more often.

'WHAT DID WE DO TODAY'
The notorious answer to the question, 'What did you do at playgroup (or nursery school) today?' is 'Nothing'. Not true of course, it just means that life went on as normal. There was the usual amount of playing with jigsaw puzzles, drawing, painting, rough and tumble, tears and giggles. But children have no concept of time passing, and find it difficult to remember what they did.

When you have a family outing, and the children are tucked up in bed afterwards, as a change from reading, talk through the exciting things that happened during the day. They will add their comments and remember things you didn't and you may learn a little of what goes in their heads, all useful for future reference and for communication between you. You may, of course, have to read a story as well, so have a short one ready!

Story game

Similar to 'My grandmother', but this involves more imagination. Start a simple story involving a character with whom the children can identify and sympathize – perhaps a favourite animal or friend, or a character from a well-known story book. The next player repeats the story so far, getting in as many details as possible, and adds the next part of the story. The third player takes over, again giving a résumé of what's gone on so far. You may never get to the end of the story, but that's not the point. Listening to the imaginative world of each child as fantasy takes flight and characters change shape and direction at will is fascinating and hilarious for all concerned.

'What was he wearing?'

This is another good party game. Dress up one child in a large number of clothes and accessories: trousers, vest (undershirt), shirt, sweater, socks, leg warmers, shoes, braces (suspenders), gloves, jacket, scarf, hat, earrings, necklaces, watch, and so on (obviously all these items must be visible in some way), until he or she is thoroughly bundled up, but not too uncomfortable. Wrap the child in a cloak and get him or her to open the cloak and appear briefly to the other children. How many items of clothing and accessories can they remember?

How many items can your children remember when you cover up the tray again?

How things work

Wheels, nuts and bolts, door handles, screws, telephones, typewriters – all gadgets we've invented to make life easier for ourselves and which we take for granted. They're all, however, a source of entertainment for children, and they are unlikely to be bored if you take the opportunities to point out how these inventions work and why we need them. You'll enjoy rediscovering these marvels and may learn something new too!

Wheels

Look out for vehicles with wheels. Cars, buses, trucks, prams (baby carriages), wheelbarrows, bicycles, motorbikes, tricycles, tractors have one, two, three or four. They are various sizes with different tracks depending on what the vehicle is used for.

Why do cars and buses have four wheels? What about a wheelbarrow? Why doesn't that have four wheels? Why not two wheels at the front? Explain that the children's toy cars and trucks work on the same principle as larger vehicles.

What would happen if wheels weren't round? (Try rolling a square building block across the table, or an egg. What's the result?)

Bicycles have two wheels. Explain that they would be much slower and less manoeuvrable if they had four.

If your child has a trike or a small two-wheeled bike, perhaps with stabilizers, show how the pedals drive the wheels which make the bike travel along.

Woodwork

If you have a piece of grassy ground that isn't in pristine condition, let very young children loose on it with a mallet with a large head and some pieces of dowelling with slightly sharpened ends. Let them bash the sticks into the ground and pull them out again.

Slightly older children can tackle real woodwork, for which you'll need to provide: pieces of scrap wood, 25 mm (1 in.), 38 mm (1½ in.), 50 mm (2 in.) nails, small saw, screws, screwdriver, sandpaper, wooden board to work on, and wooden wheels.

Show children, with the help of the wooden board, how to use tools properly. Provide small proper tools rather than toy ones. It's a good idea to practise hammering into chunks of potato to start with and to saw up corrugated cardboard until a good sawing technique is mastered.

Safety notes
Tiny fingers can get horribly trapped under hammers, in bolts, even in the telephone dial. Make sure the children know how to use tools properly before letting them loose with them, and always keep a close watch. Children using sewing machines need careful supervision. Do not start any activity with any of these objects unless you are going to be with the children all the time.

Get the children to study the pieces of wood. What could they make with them? Go along with their suggestions and be encouraging whenever possible. If you think they have an unworkable idea, talk it through carefully until they see why that is so.

Machines

Try to get hold of a secondhand office adding machine. It's got great play value. A solid old typewriter, preferably one which rings a bell when you get to the end of the line, is good for a bash too. You can show how the keys work the hammers which make marks on the paper.

An old hand-operated sewing machine is a better investment than a toy version as it is sturdier and less frustrating. Show the children how to operate it, give them a few scraps of material and some scissors and suggest they use the sewing machine to make something.

Mechanics board

Attach to a large piece of wood a bolt, a telephone handle with cord which they can take off a hook, a zip, screws with nuts, a door handle, an old lock and a large hook and eye so the children can fiddle whenever they feel inclined. Add a few dowels and provide wool which can be wound round in a pattern.

Attach the board to a wall, at a child-size height.

Playing with a mechanics board like this satisfies children's natural curiosity in everyday gadgets and helps them discover for themselves 'how things work'.

Experiments in science

Children are natural scientists. They harbour a curiosity which many of us lose as we grow up. Those endless questions (Why? How? When? Where?) may sometimes get you down, but they do provide the chance to talk about the application of scientific principles in the house and on the street, and even to carry out some experiments at home. The ideas here are only starting points, and you will be guided by their questions and what interests them. A lot of adults are frightened by the word 'science', but remember it's a word that covers such everyday things as turning on a light switch or cooking.

Horseshoe magnets are cheap and good value for scientific experiments – like fishing!

Magnets

You really need a small horseshoe magnet for each child, otherwise there will be fights. To start with just let them play with these, picking up whatever they can on the end. They can make two piles of objects – those things that are attracted to the magnet, and those that can't be picked up (include coins and other metal objects that aren't attracted to magnets). Let them see if the magnet will work through paper, cardboard or wood.

A good magic trick is to drop a paperclip or metal screw into a glass of water and ask the children if they can remove the object without getting wet. This can be done by sliding a magnet carefully under the glass until it engages with the object, then bringing it slowly up the side to the top of the glass. If you hold a magnet under a table or a tray, or a piece of cardboard, can you move the metal objects lying on top?

Then try the magnetized fishing game. Cut out fish from pieces of coloured paper and slide a large-sized paperclip on to the side of each one. Put these in a bowl. Make fishing rods from sticks and string with small horseshoe magnets attached to the end. Put the fish in the bowl, equip each child with a fishing rod and see who catches the most fish.

Electricity

Children soon learn that the vacuum cleaner won't work unless you plug it in and switch it on, and that the room remains dark in the evening until you turn the light on. They may not realize that the same force makes both these things work. Show them the fuse box (if possible, switch off a circuit to show how some lights will go out), point out the wires coming into the house, explain how the electricity meter works. Of course, they must *never* fiddle with these things on their own. Explain why. But you can let them help you turn a light on or off.

Take out the battery from a battery-operated toy and show how it no longer works. Explain that the battery provides electrical power too.

Plumbing

Shut off the water mains for a few minutes to show that the water in the tap is not limitless. Explain that it is piped to your home through a complicated collection of pipes going under your street and under your town and that the whole lot is interconnected. Waste water is taken away in another series of pipes. One child was fascinated by the water going down the plughole from his bath and decided it went to 'the waterman'.

Street science

Especially in winter, children often notice for themselves that the street lights go on and off. Explain that this is organized at a central electricity station, using a much bigger version of your own fuse box at home.

Keep an eye out for asphalting. Watch the men mixing it up, spreading it on the road, smoothing it over. Observe the strong smell and colour. On hot days, new asphalt gets soft and sticky.

Pneumatic drills, cranes and dump trucks, men working on electricity cables or water pipes, a window cleaner on a scaffolding moving up and down a huge building by means of a pulley, are all good reasons for you and the children to stop and have a conversation.

COOKING

Strange things happen to the ingredients in a cake when they are mixed together and cooked. It's easy for us to take these changes for granted, but for children it's a magical business.

Let the children help right from the beginning. Line up the ingredients. Let them weigh, sift, chop, mix and taste; help them to hold the electric whisk if necessary. The mixture that goes into the oven takes up far less space than the finished cake and its consistency, smell and taste are quite different.

Safety notes

Any observation of electrical equipment should take place *only* under your supervision, and never let the children play with plugs.

39

Modelling

Playing with clay and playdough is wonderfully therapeutic. 'Modelling' allows the imagination to run riot and to experience the special qualities of these cool and malleable materials that change shape so easily. A child absorbed with modelling is a happy child indeed, and should be given plenty of time to make discoveries.

Clay

Craft suppliers sell ordinary modelling clay ready-mixed; it has to be kept in polythene in an airtight container, and be mixed and kneaded with water quite regularly, as it tends to dry out in hot little hands and when it is stored.

Some children – usually older ones – find clay more exciting than dough or Plasticine, though it is messy. The wetter the clay the better, and the more possibilities there are for creative play. It can be prodded, almost liquidized for smoothing over, slapped about and slopped down on the table in a very satisfactory way. Some children will enjoy just running their hands over the surface of a ball of clay, digging their fingers and nails into it. Others will want to make real models. However, many children find it hard to work and get frustrated when they cannot do anything. Don't persevere if they find it hard going.

Papier mâché

Another messy material, this is nevertheless fun, cheap and easy to use. It sets surprisingly hard, and models made with it will last for years.

Tear up several newspapers into little pieces or strips (keep the strips for use as a final wrapping around larger items, like animals and heads, for example) and soak them in a big bowl of hot water until they are very soft and ready to break up. Then take out the paper with your hands and squeeze it out. Rub it into a pulp. Put this into a cloth and wring it until every scrap of moisture has gone. Now mix this with cooled home-made paste (see page 18). Treat papier mâché like thick clay. It can't go in the oven, of course, but it can be painted.

Plasticine

This is less satisfactory than playdough or clay because it is hard to warm in the hands and soften enough to be really malleable. But it is a good standby and comes in lots of different colours.

MAKING PLAYDOUGH

Although this is available commercially, it's cheaper to make at home.

The following dough recipe has a good texture and can either be stored for reuse or cooked, left to cool and painted.

450 g (1 lb./4 cups) self-raising (all-purpose) flour
100 g (4 oz./1 cup) salt
powder paint to colour (optional)
water to mix

Mix the ingredients together with just enough water to make the dough malleable, but not too soft. You can keep it usable for a few days by putting it in a polythene bag in the fridge or an airtight container.

Playdough lacks some of the qualities of clay – it is more stable and more predictable – but it is very useful for younger children.

Starting to model

A few tools such as pastry cutters, rolling pins, lollipop (popsicle) sticks or other prodding accessories can be helpful, but don't always put these out and make sure the children are thoroughly familiar with the clay or playdough before you offer them.

Resist the temptation to show the children how you would do it. If you, at your first attempt, make a perfect giraffe or dinosaur, they may become very discouraged. Play with them, by all means, but make your experiments joint discussions. Ask their advice and only give yours if you're asked for an opinion.

Animals, little people, cups, saucers and dishes can all be fashioned with thumbs and fingers. Dishes can also be made by pressing a china or plastic doll's teaset bowl into a ball of clay to get a good shape. Older children may like to roll out their clay or playdough into a long, thinnish sausage and use a length to coil a small pot. The inside and outside can then be smoothed with thumbs and fingers as before. You'll need water to smooth clay into shape.

Designs can be made with the tools. Abstract patterns are best. Favourite clay models can be baked in a hot oven and the finished bits and pieces painted and decorated. (Some clay models may spring apart at the neck in the oven if the children haven't used enough watery clay to join two lumps together.)

Poster paint is the best for decorating both playdough and clay models. Make sure they are dry first. Be sure to appreciate dishes given to you as presents and if at all possible *use* them for something!

A lump of dough and a few 'tools' provide plenty of scope for the imagination.

Playing shop

Playing shop is not just learning about money, though that is important; it is also an opportunity to act out a grown-up situation, and is valuable fantasy play. The 'shop' may well develop into a small-scale 'factory', where the goods are made and sold on the premises, or a social situation, where the customer is invited to look after the shop while the shopkeeper goes for a walk with the dog, for instance. Playing shop offers endless possibilities of this kind.

Before they can understand how we count money, children need to get the idea of buying and selling.

Role play

Setting up a shop at home with priced items is a useful prop. Give the children some toy money, and a shopping bag each, and see what develops. Not only will the children begin to understand the value of money, they will also get a chance to play out adult niceties and indulge in social 'small talk'.

While they're enjoying themselves handing over money and receiving change, they are likely to mimic the conversations they've heard between supermarket cashier and customer – 'Good morning', 'Nice weather we're having', 'Thanks a lot', 'Have a nice day!', 'See you later'. You'll undoubtedly recognize yourself in these exchanges!

'Where do I buy...?'

Have a few items ready – different kinds of food, clothes, a hammer or other tools, books, stationery – and suggest that each child represents a different kind of shop: supermarket, deli, hardware store, clothes shop, bookshop and so on.

Hold up an item. Who should have it in their shop? That child comes and collects the item.

Sorting coins

What a complicated business money is! For a start, there are so many coins, all of which look very alike to children. A little help is in order.

Keep a pile of small change for the children to play with, so they become familiar with coins. Tell them what each coin is and let them sort out the collection into separate piles. They'll soon learn the names and get the idea that some coins are more valuable than others.

MAKING A MONEY CHART
Once a week, or whenever you have a fair amount of change around the house, help the children make a chart. Label columns with the names of all the coins you have, and let the children draw coins in these columns to represent the number of real ones. They can colour in the coins appropriately if they like. If they are beginning to learn to count, help them work out whether you have more of one coin or another than you did the week before.

At the supermarket

On a shopping trip, let the children help you find the things you want to buy, pick them up and put them carefully in the trolley. It may seem to make the shopping trip longer, but they will learn a lot about grouping and sorting, and it will help to prevent them getting bored. All the cereals are together, the jams (jellies) and preserves, frozen foods, and so on. Gradually they will recognize the names of goods too, which will help their reading.

At the same time, point out the marked price of anything you buy and explain that you have brought money with you to pay for your food and drink. As they get older they will recognize the numbers and be able to tell you how much an item costs. If you are only buying a few items with cash, they may be able to help you sort out money from your purse to pay for your purchases.

Pocket money

A little regular pocket money out of which children can buy their own treats and treasures helps teach them the value of money and that, once it is spent, it cannot, unfortunately, be spent again!

Making decisions, buying, selling, exchanging money, having a conversation – playing shop is a good way for children to explore the adult world.

Sewing, weaving and threading

Sewing can be a bit tricky for a young child. Manipulating a needle, coping with thread, getting those stitches in the right place, and going in the direction they want is a tall order. But it's a creative activity, and a finished piece of sewing or weaving is something to be proud of. So keep projects simple and make plenty of encouraging noises over the children's first efforts.

Sewing cards

Make (or buy) some sewing cards. Equip the children with a darning needle each, and help them thread the needle with coloured wool (talk about colours while you're doing this). Double the thread, so that the needle stays threaded, and tie a knot in the end. Their job is to weave the needle and wool in and out along the lines until they have completed the shape on the card.

You can do this with the children's names too. The cards can then be hung on the bedroom door.

Four- and five-year-olds might like to try 'dot-to-dotting'. You suggest the image on the card with strategically placed needle holes, numbered, and the children join these up to make a 'surprise' picture.

Making 'gloves'

Ask the children to draw around their own hands on to paper and cut out the shapes, leaving as much paper round the hand shapes as they can when they cut. These patterns can then be pinned on to some double-thickness, brightly coloured, scrap material and cut out. This will give four hand-shapes.

The two pattern pieces for each hand can then be pinned and sewn together with running stitch all the way round (leaving holes big enough for small hands). The 'gloves' can then be turned inside out. They may not last long but will be shown off proudly to friends and relatives.

More threading

All kinds of household cast-offs make good threading material – foil bottle tops, yoghurt carton tops, chopped-up straws, small felt shapes, sequins, beads, buttons. As a general rule, use larger objects for small children. For the thread, use a large-eyed darning needle with string or strong wool.

MAKING SEWING CARDS

1 Cut some thin card into squares.
2 On these, draw some large, simple shapes or pictures (cat, dog, familiar toy) in stylized, angular form.
3 Push a needle through at various points on the straight lines, not too far apart.

44

A card for threading and tying is a useful prop for shoelace practice.

WEAVING

Weaving is fun for children of all ages, and can be started very simply at three or four years old.

1 Take a shoebox and punch six holes in each end. Then take three pieces of wool or string, each long enough to be doubled through the holes in the box and tied at one end.

2 Next, take another piece of wool, wind it round a piece of cardboard and let the children thread this under and over the wool in the shoebox. Show them how to keep the weaving neat.

3 When one piece of wool is finished, they can move on to another, knot it to the first and make a striped piece of material that can be sewn up into a little purse or a wristband.

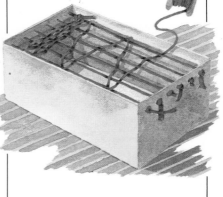

Snake-like toys, bangles, headbands, wall hangings – the decorative possibilities of threading are endless. Shiny foil bottle or carton tops threaded together on a string and hung in the garden may attract magpies.

Threading and tying shoelaces

Their teachers will be delighted if your children know how to tie their own shoelaces when they start school. Most children need masses of practice.

Find an old discarded trainer or sneaker, give it a coat or two with a felt tip pen and thread it with a brightly coloured shoelace for the children to tie and untie.

Alternatively, draw a shoe on a piece of card, cut it out, punch holes in it and use that instead.

Straw weaving

Find some paper straws (not plastic), flatten them and weave them together to make table mats or hanging decorations.

Safety notes

Two- and three-year-olds are likely to try and eat small beads, so give them larger ones to play with. Do make sure that needles are the blunt-ended, darning type, and that your children know how to use scissors (the round-ended variety) correctly.

Making music

Listening to music cheers you up, calms you down, encourages dreams and fantasies, echoes your mood, makes you want to dance. It's never too early to introduce children to the joys of pop, classical, jazz, folk and reggae music – each has its own special magic to offer. A good mixture introduces ideas of different rhythms, tempos, types of singing, and the music of other cultures and past centuries. Music is another language, and a good understanding and love of it will enrich anybody's life.

ACTION RHYMES

The familiar repetition and rhyming of action songs helps children remember what's coming next. Here are two popular ones:

I'm a little teapot, short and stout,
Here's my handle, here's my
    spout,
When the kettle's boiling, hear
    me shout,
Tip me up and pour me out!

I can reach up to the sky,
I can crouch down on the floor,
I can twirl around and around,
And still walk straight through the
    door.

'One finger, one thumb, keep moving...' Action rhymes are popular, especially with groups of children.

Learning to listen

This doesn't mean music lessons from year one, though some children do respond well to early training. Many, though, have trouble concentrating for longer than a few minutes, so anything that can help them to extend that period will stand them in good stead at school and later in life. Listening to sounds and learning to distinguish between them is an excellent exercise.

Start by filling one jar with dried peas and another with dried butter beans. When you shake the peas jar it will make a higher, shriller noise than the butter beans jar. Get the children to cover their eyes and to call out 'peas' or 'butter beans' when you rattle one of the jars. They will be eager to shake the jars themselves, too.

Try this exercise with other objects such as a bunch of keys and a jar of coffee beans.

Explain 'high' and 'low' notes. Sing, hum, strum an instrument, playing two notes at a time, one high, one low (you need no musical training to do this!) and ask the children to say which is which. Then play one loud and one soft, and again ask the children to distinguish them. Get them to sing loud, sing soft, to whisper and to shout – many children need little encouragement to shout!

First steps with music

Clap a *very* simple rhythm (ta, ta-ta taaaaa) and get the children to clap it back to you. Progress gradually until the rhythm is more complicated. Then, if you feel confident enough, sing or play a simple tune (just a few notes you can make up on a xylophone, whistle or recorder). Can the children sing it back to you? Some find this easy, others can't do it at all to start with, but will improve with practice.

Dancing to music

Play various kinds of music on a tape recorder – marches, waltzes, pop, jazz – and ask the children to improvise a dance to suit each piece: slow and sad, quick and jolly, like a soldier, like a tramp, like a scarecrow, and so on. It's best if they do this one by one to start with, otherwise the less confident will copy the older more extrovert children. But don't push the reluctant to join in.

Making musical instruments

You can use the pea and bean instruments you made (above), and bring into play pots, pans, frying pans, wooden spoons, ordinary spoons, kitchen implements, foil tops in a plastic bag (for maracas), plastic boxes. Let the children bang away and take turns with favourite pieces of equipment.

Many stores stock good quality 'toy' instruments, such as recorders, whistles, drums, xylophones and tambourines. These will always be a welcome addition to your children's band.

A comb and a piece of paper make a good blowing instrument, and rubber bands stretched between nails hammered into a piece of wood make a good apparatus for twanging. A bottle octave (right) is a good instrument to bang.

MAKING A BOTTLE OCTAVE

1 If you have a good ear (you'll have to check the bottles against a musical instrument), fill eight bottles of the same size to different levels with water (to make an octave).
2 Give the children a wooden spoon each and let them try to play a simple tune by banging the bottles. Here is the sequence for 'Ba-ba Black Sheep', using eight bottles.
1, 1, 5, 5, 6, 7, 8, 6, 5,
4, 4, 3, 3, 2, 2, 1,
5, 5, 5, 4, 4, 4, 3, 3, 3, 2,
5, 5, 5, 4, 5, 6, 4, 3, 2, 2, 1.

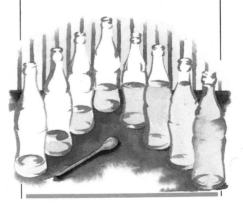

Look after your body

A tiny baby will gaze for hours at its hands and feet, play with its toes, clap hands and pull at your face. And the human body after all is a weird and wonderful piece of equipment. Learning a little about how it works, how it helps you walk and run, sit and lie and how it reflects feelings makes for some interesting and often hilarious experiments.

Dancing
Dancing to music (see page 47) is an excellent way of getting children to move their bodies unselfconsciously, as well as requiring minimum encouragement. Get them to dance with different parts of their bodies. 'Let your arms dance…now your feet…now wiggle your bottom…shake your tummy' and so on. They'll learn different movements and exercise new muscles.

Exercises
Ask the children to sit with their legs astride, and backs straight, and then bend down to the floor. Rare is the child who cannot get his or her chest flat on the floor. Now you try it. Unless you're very supple, the chances are you'll hardly be able to move from the vertical.

It's a shame to let children stiffen up as they grow older. The answer is to exercise regularly. Gym classes for very young children are increasingly common. Make sure that the teachers are qualified and the exercises not too strenuous. Otherwise, why not start up a regular exercise class of your own at home, just you and the children. Work to music. Stretch right up, touch toes, bend sideways, squat, swing legs, raise feet off the ground to tighten tummy muscles, run and jump on the spot. They'll enjoy getting puffed out.

Try and set aside about 15 minutes three times a week, preferably in the morning when no-one is too tired to join in.

Pushing and pulling involves the children sitting in a see-saw position, opposite each other, legs bent, holding hands. They then push and pull to the tune of 'See-saw, marjory daw'.

Somersaults and handstands take confidence. Put cushions on the floor and help the children turn head over heels. Some four- and five-year-olds are ready to do handstands against a wall. How does the world look upside-down? What can they see? Do they feel dizzy?

Swimming

Swimming is the best exercise for everyone, as it works the muscles but gently supports them in the water so that injury is very unlikely. Take the children swimming from babyhood onwards, though if they're frightened cuddle them in the water and be prepared to take them out if they become unhappy. Little and often is best!

Gradually they'll be able to float off in armbands or other supports – D-shaped armbands are the best; they are comfortable and you can gradually let down the air as the children gain confidence – and start kicking. Many children who go to a pool regularly can swim before they start school. Swimming is good fun, an excellent family activity, therapeutic and good for building up muscles and confidence.

Making faces

Sit down with your children and get them to imitate a whole range of facial expressions. Screw up your eyes, wrinkle your nose, drop your jaw to your chest, roll your eyes, open your mouth wide, smile, frown, stick out your tongue as far as it will go. This is good for the facial muscles and likely to end in a good giggle.

Can the children make an angry face, a sad face, a happy face? Let them have a go and then look in the mirror. Can they improve on their first efforts?

Left: *A tug of war see-saw is good fun and strengthens arms, legs and tummies.*

Below: *Encourage your children to enjoy water. Swimming is the best exercise for everyone.*

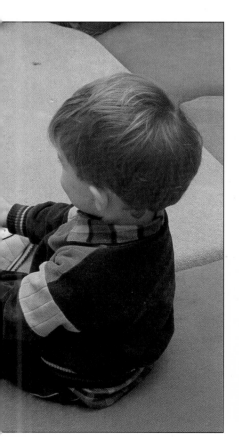

Get knitting!

Knitting has become a fashionable activity again for all ages – and both sexes. And a pair of big needles and a box full of wool odds and ends can be great fun for pre-school children. It's good for their concentration and co-ordination and, when an item, no matter how small or simple, is finished, it's a matter of great pride. Some four- and five-year-olds may be able to knit simple garments after just a few sessions practising with scraps of wool and needles (but younger than that they are unlikely to have the co-ordination).

Starting off
Choose big needles and thick wool. It is best if you do the casting on to start with. Cast on about 10 stitches and explain how to do 'knit'. 'Purl' needs more dexterity, and is probably best left until they are confident of their ability.

The children are bound to drop stitches and get frustrated, so sit by them and help for the first two or three rows, then see how they get on. Even a small piece of knitting 10 stitches wide by 10 rows deep can be folded up and sewn into a purse.

Patchwork squares
If you have several children to work with, get them all going on squares. This means they must all have the same size needles and also the same kind of wool in different colours. Get them to knit squares 20 stitches across and 20 rows deep, though expect a wide variation in the size of squares they produce.

You can then sew these together to make a doll's blanket or a lining for a dog basket, or a bag to keep your wool in.

Doll's scarves
Child-size scarves are far too much work for one child, though several can team up to knit lengths that can be joined later. Alternatively, you could help out with a few rows now and then.

One child should be able to manage a length of knitting that will keep a doll warm, and it won't take very long to make. Show the children how to make stripes in the scarf. When knitting in stripes, they should always knit an even number of rows in each colour (this makes the changeover rows much neater).

SAUSAGE ANIMALS
These can be made very easily with lengths of garter stitch. This pattern is for a snake, but it could just as easily be a worm or a caterpillar. Simply change the stripes as the children see fit. You will probably have to be on hand for casting on and off, and for those rows where a stitch should be increased or decreased. Also, some children may get fed up and want you to do a few rows to help them out.

You'll need:
two 50 g (2 oz.) balls of double knitting (worsted) wool in different colours
cottonwool (absorbent cotton) or kapok

1 Cast on 24 stitches. Knit 8 rows in Colour A, increasing one stitch at the beginning of every row. Then knit 10 rows without increasing.
2 The stripes are formed by knitting 4 rows in Colour B and 8 rows in Colour A six times altogether. Finish with an extra 4 rows in Colour B. To make an extra long snake or wriggly worm, repeat the striped section a few more times.
3 Using colour A knit 10 rows. Then knit 8 rows, knitting 2 stitches together at the beginning of each row to decrease. Cast off.
4 Fold the snake in half inside out. Sew the edges together, but leave a hole for the stuffing. Sew across the corners in a curve. Turn snake right side out and stuff him with cottonwool, kapok or old tights.

'I knit one, Grandma knits one...' making a knitted square is not too difficult for older pre-schoolers.

50

Other ideas

'Jewellery' is very easily made. A length of knitting, just 4 stitches wide, will soon provide a necklace, or a matching bracelet, or even a tiny ring. A length of 6 stitches wide will make a headband or wristband.

Larger squares can be made into leg warmers. Sew up the sides, then simply help the children thread a darning needle with shirring elastic (elastic thread) and weave it through both ends (see Sewing, weaving and threading, pages 44-5). Omit the elastic and you have a muff!

Jigsaw puzzles

Jigsaw puzzles are an old and unfailing favourite, and also provide excellent practice for reading. The concentration involved in working out what shape fits which hole, while keeping an eye on the complete picture, uses similar skills.

They are also an absorbing family activity and as children get older they will enjoy sitting round a jigsaw table with brothers and sisters working on a very demanding commercial puzzle. To start with, though, the puzzles must be simple, with very few pieces.

First steps

Cut out simple pictures, with square edges, from old greeting cards or books and stick them on some stiff, but cuttable card. Leave a border round the edge to mark corners and borders. You will need a sharp craft knife to cut the picture into four or at the most six pieces. Make some curved, and some straight, lines, but nothing too complicated at this stage. Now let the child fit them together.

This is not as easy as it looks. Not only do left and right have to be sorted out, but back and front and right side up too.

As the children gain confidence, increase the size of the picture and/or the number of pieces, but don't make the shapes too complicated.

Matching picture cards

You'll need about 20 picture cards, cut in half, some lengthwise, some horizontally, and with neatly cut jagged edges. Only the correct halves will fit together. Spread these out face up on the floor or table and let the children puzzle out the pictures.

The next stage, for four- and five-year-olds, is to turn the cards face down and let the children try to match them without pictures. Only give them two or three cards at a time.

Word jigsaw puzzles

Write a few familiar words on a sheet of paper and match them with a drawing or magazine picture describing the word. Cut them out and stick them on card. Cut a line with a sharp craft knife between the word and picture. The children then try to match up the two halves. They will soon start to take account of the word and its picture rather than simply noticing the pattern of the shapes.

THREE-DIMENSIONAL JIGSAW PUZZLES

Break a papier mâché pot, preferably into four or five largish pieces, and ask the children's help in putting it together again. This activity involves a slightly different skill as the children have to think on more than one plane. The pot can be glued together with an all-purpose adhesive.

Try two words that are linked in some way: for example, tree and leaf, flower and petal, cup and saucer, bread and jam (jelly). Stick each pair on a piece of card and cut out as before.

Parts of the body

Get the children to lie down on pieces of thick lining paper or newsprint and draw round each other. They can then fill in the outline with face, hair, clothes, shoes, gloves, and so on.

Label the parts of the body in thick felt-tip pen: arm, leg, head, stomach, chest, feet, toes, hands, fingers, elbows, knees, neck, ears.

You then cut the bodies out carefully into several pieces (each child can puzzle out his or her own shape so adjust the number and shape of the pieces to the age of the child) and let the children put themselves together again on the floor. It doesn't matter whether or not you cut through the labelling. This is a good way to learn the parts of the body as well as create a jigsaw puzzle.

Lethargic and easy-going dogs can be puzzled out in the same way. Cats are less accommodating!

Commercial jigsaw puzzles

There are cheerful, simple jigsaw puzzles on the market, some of which are designed for the floor, with giant pieces and bright colours. Once the children are happy doing these, move on to smaller puzzles, again with only a few pieces. Anything bigger than a 20-piece puzzle will need your close co-operation.

There's no need to buy jigsaws for the very young. Simple ones can be made from greeting cards, postcards or small posters.

Loving books

Books are real treasure troves: so much to dream and fantasize about, so many attractive characters to identify with, those funny sounding words and interesting squiggles on the page, such beautiful pictures.

Some children take to books and reading easily, constantly demanding from a very early age to be read to and then to be told what such and such a word says. Others show no interest or motivation until they get to school and have been there a term or two and suddenly realize *why* people bother to read, and then there's no stopping them. Some need more help.

At the age of three or four, looking at books together, reading aloud and enjoying some activities that prepare children for reading – jigsaw puzzles (see pages 52-3) or memory games (pages 34-5) for instance – are all you need do. Even more important are the experience of language, the rhythm of words, the pattern of print on a page, and the huge richness of our vocabulary. There is no need to give 'reading lessons' or make the business a chore; in fact, these will be counterproductive. Children learn so much while they're playing with you or with each other and listening to you reading to them. All they need are a little encouragement and a few props.

Reading aloud

This is the most important thing you can do to foster a love of books, as well as being infallible entertainment for the children. Curl up comfortably together in a chair or on the bed and look at books as often as you can. Make it a warm and cosy occasion and choose a time when you are both relaxed.

Let the children look at the book and ask questions. Try not to complain if it's the same story every night. Some children memorize books from start to finish, and will imitate the cadence of a sentence and the rhythm of speech they hear from you, as well as anticipating the plot and elaborating on the storyline. That's all worth while.

Point out the pictures and ask questions about them.

Trace the words with your finger as you read them, to show that writing starts at the top left of a page and ends bottom right. This is something adults take for granted, but children find it difficult to understand how you can make a story out of a mass of confused black scribbles on a page.

WORDS AND MORE WORDS
Young babies respond to the sound of the human voice, and even though they can't understand the meaning of what you say, they quickly realize that language plays a very important part in communication.

Talk to your children as much as possible, and get them to talk to you. Listen, make comments, ask questions, and encourage them to describe things and events in detail. Use interesting, strange words that they will want to roll around their tongue and say themselves.

The bee buzzed busily
While the wasp whizzed wheezily
And the helicopter whirred in the
  sky

The bird trilled merrily
While the plane zoomed
  zingingly
Why oh why can't I fly?

Shapes and colours

Letters and words on a page make a pattern, as do triangles, circles, squares and cylinders. So learning to differentiate between these shapes is good practice for distinguishing letters.

Start with one shape and find as many things as you can that are square or round. Gradually add others until they are shape-perfect.

Do your children recognize colours? Let them draw the shapes they know on a page and colour them in. Write the names of the colours with the appropriate crayon or felt tip next to the shapes.

Making picture books

This is a good way to interest a child reluctant to look at books. Make your own, containing pictures and words which have some personal meaning: 'What I do at playgroup', or 'My dog' or 'My back yard', for instance. Keep sentences short and simple and always print clearly in lower case letters, not capitals (except for the first letter in proper names). Read these aloud to your children like an ordinary book. Don't insist they 'read' the words.

There are some more ideas for reading games and activities on pages 56-7.

RHYMES

Rhymes are a good way to remember new and interesting words. There are plenty of paperback poetry books for young children, or you could make up a few simple rhymes yourself. Read them as many times as your children want. This may be every night at bedtime for a couple of weeks, so choose poems that you like yourself! Write out favourites in large letters on a big sheet of paper and put them on the bedroom wall. Your children won't *read* them, but they will begin to recognize the pattern of the words and will pounce on them when they appear in a picture story book.

Rhymes with actions to go with them are also good memory joggers. Here's a favourite:

Incy Wincy Spider
Climbing up the spout
Down came the rain and
Washed poor Incy out
Out came the sunshine
And dried up all the rain
Then Incy Wincy Spider
Climbed up the spout again.

Make sure you set aside a quiet time every day to look at books with your child.

Learning to read

Appreciating language and the magic of books is the first step towards reading. It's a natural progression from looking at pictures and listening to you reading aloud to picking out words, and most children are enthusiastic about games and activities that show the relationship between objects and the written words that describe them.

Labelling

Although looking at complete books is considered the best way for children to begin to learn to read, you can help reading skills in other ways. It might make a mess of your decorative scheme, but labelling objects around the house and putting name-plates above pegs or around the table at some meals is an excellent way of familiarizing children with words. Fridge, kettle, cooker, mirror, picture, chair, table, door, window, television, telephone, all crop up regularly in conversation and children's books. Don't worry about some words being long. Familiar words with several letters are just as easy to recognize as 'cat' and 'dog'.

Label the children's drawings and paintings with the title they want.

Picture charts

Pick on an everyday subject such as the weather, the time, the days of the week, your children's friends, your family, for drawing and matching words. For instance, pictures to represent a sunny day, rain, storm or clouds can be paired up with the appropriate words. Each day ask your child to pin up the appropriate picture and label on the wall. For friends and family, write names and ask the children to draw pictures of each person concerned. Pair up the picture with the label. For the days of the week, pick on an activity you always do on a particular day (see also pages 20-1 on time). Write the name of the day on one card and draw a picture to represent the activity on another.

Picture/word snap

This is a good game for children who can already recognize a few words.

Make a set of, say, 20 cards. On ten of these draw familiar people, objects or toys and on the other ten write the word to describe them. Two people play. One person has the picture cards, the other the words, and they put them down in two piles alternately. Shout 'Snap' when a word matches a picture.

Notes

1 Remember to use the library. Let the children browse around and choose books to interest them.
2 Keep telling stories and reading aloud for several years after your children are reading for themselves.
3 Never insist that a child reads a book so that you can clock up a particular number. Reading ability should never be competitive.

Giving children plenty of opportunity to practise making their mark is the best preparation for writing, although four- and five-year-olds might enjoy copying a few familiar words.

Writing

As soon as a young child can hold a crayon, he or she seems compelled to make a mark on the world – or at least on the bedroom walls! Gradually what looks like scribble to adult eyes will develop into a form of writing that contains shapes resembling letters. All you need to do at this stage is provide a range of writing tools, thick and thin, and encourage experiments. Writing is a difficult craft and it's essential not to put children off by getting them to copy letters in any formal way. Answer questions and give advice and help when it is asked for. It is helpful to teachers if children know how to hold and manipulate a pencil when they start school.

Bedroom blackboard

If you have the space, paint a large piece of hardboard with matt black paint, attach it to the children's bedroom wall and supply a box of coloured chalk. They can use this for scribbling on, but you can keep one part of it for writing words – just one or two at a time and ones they are likely to recognize, such as bed, toothbrush, cup, drink, teddy, doll, book, hot, cold. Leave a space underneath each word in case they want to try to copy them, but don't force this.

Action words

For a small group of children who have started to read, make some word cards with the names of actions on them: run, jump, dance, kick, walk, clap, sing, turn around, stamp, whistle, shout, and so on. Put the cards face down in the middle of the room. Each child picks up a card in turn and does whatever it says.

Keeping pets

Grown-ups are so accustomed to pets that it's easy to forget that in some ways they are more exciting to children than wild animals in a safari park or a zoo. There, the animals are behind fences or enclosures; there is little or no contact between child and animal. But a dog, hamster, rabbit or gerbil is very much a friend. Its survival depends on you and your children feeding it, providing it with shelter and warmth and playing with it. Children younger than five can enjoy these pets, but before that age they cannot be expected to take much responsibility for their welfare.

Bringing any pet into the home does mean that you will ultimately be responsible for it. It is too much to expect a young child to do everything without being told when and how to do it, and without being offered some help and support. You are also taking on a financial cost, for vets' (veterinarian's) charges for illness and for operations like spaying a cat.

Not only do pets bind you to the house, the caged varieties also have a way of escaping and getting lost. This invariably causes much *angst* in the family and means that *you* will be crouching by the hole under the fridge waiting for an errant hamster to emerge while the children cry themselves to sleep upstairs. Pets in and around the house, however, are a great pleasure for children, and taking care of weaker creatures is a skill worth fostering.

If you are not sure whether or not you want to take on a pet, why not borrow one from a friend going on holiday or a nursery school near you?

Choosing a pet
Rabbits and guinea pigs need regular exercise in a garden, so if you have no garden go for hamsters, gerbils, rats or mice. A cat is probably the least trouble, since it looks after itself except for food, milk and water, whereas a dog can be as demanding as a small child.

Look into the question of care and feeding before you buy a pet. Also check up on housing requirements and breeding possibilities.

Before you buy the pet, get a simple book on looking after it and look through it with your children, explaining all the things you will need to do together to keep the animal happy. Then take your children along to the pet shop and let them choose the animal they like best, look for the right food, and choose a cage and any toys or other bits and pieces the animal will need.

Safety notes
It is very important to make sure hamsters and gerbils, in particular, do not escape since if they breed in the wild they can cause great damage to crops. Any animal is likely to scratch if handled roughly or clumsily.

58

Taming your pet

Whatever animal you decide to have, it is important that the children should handle it a little two or three times a day, so that it knows they are friends. Don't let them shout or speak loudly near the cage or hutch, but always approach quietly and make slow movements. If you have a rowdy toddler, stress the importance of restrained behaviour. Dogs, of course, must be taken for regular walks.

Enjoying your pet

Observe your pet together. What does it look like? Can you describe it? What colour is it? What colour are its eyes? What do its ears look like? Is its fur long or short, rough or smooth? How does it move? Does it hop, jump, scamper, crawl, run? How does it sleep – in a heap, stretched out? Can you see it breathing? How does it eat? How does it wash itself? Does it hold its food in its paws or eat out of a dish?

Feeding and housing

A pet shop will give you instructions on feeding and cleaning out. Clean, dry bedding for all pets is essential as is a healthy diet. Rabbits and guinea pigs need a run attached to their hutches in the garden for exercise. Guinea pigs need to be brought indoors in winter. Gerbils, hamsters, rats and mice should be kept indoors or in a well-insulated garden shed.

Having a pet around the house helps children learn that where animals are concerned a gentle approach and a certain amount of respect pay off.

Garden adventures

Not everyone is lucky enough to have a garden, but if you do have access to a private patch, or if your children's playgroup, day care centre, or nursery school has a garden, it can be turned into another playroom with the added advantage of fresh air and healthy exercise.

The smallest garden can be a jumping-off point for all kinds of fantasy games involving cowboys and Indians, jungle crawling or shipwreck survivors, as well as the more ordinary games of tag or hide and seek.

Tent adventure

Dens of any kind are a great delight – a secret hidey-hole to crawl away from the world and create a special fantasy world. For a reasonably sized garden, a tent makes an ideal den. A sunny or at least dry day is essential, or you'll find you've no sooner put up the tent than you have to take it down again.

Involve the children in putting up the tent, helping them sort out the poles and guy ropes, and counting the tent pegs. A big wooden mallet is useful for banging in tent pegs (but make sure the children keep their fingers well away from the pegs). Apart from the practical things to consider for the tent – sleeping bags, washing-up bowl, cooking equipment, rugs, picnic stuff – your children will have ideas of their own – dolls, teddies, books, and so on.

If you're feeling bold and the suggestion comes from the children, you could sleep out together on a warm night, and cook supper on a camping stove outside the tent.

Obstacle course

Fix up a mini assault course with a rope hanging from a tree to swing on, some tree trunks to walk over, and old, washed plastic dustbins with the bottoms cut out to make tunnels. These can lead into a den made out of a tent, branches or a sheet hung over garden chairs.

Fix up a plank supported over a paddling pool. Don't make it too high, of course, but the children must balance if they don't want to get their feet wet.

Suggest jungle games, such as one child stalking another. It's surprising how small children can make themselves invisible in even a miniature garden. Slithering along on one's stomach like a snake is the most inconspicuous way to make progress.

Safety notes

For some children the outdoors spells grazes, cuts and other minor disasters. Be prepared with a first-aid kit, containing plasters, scissors and antiseptic lotion or cream. If you light a fire, make sure they understand the dangers of it and keep well back.

Modified tree house

A real tree house is a major undertaking and probably only worth doing as the children get a bit older. But as an interim arrangement you could make a wooden platform set on stilts about 60 cm (2 ft) off the ground, banked up with branches to make walls and a roof. A small ladder and an old curtain for the front door make a perfect private hideaway.

The children can use it as an outside playhouse and take in whatever toys and equipment they like.

Garden toys

There are plenty of attractive garden toys on the market. Swings, slides, see-saws, plastic tunnelling equipment, trampolines, and high-jumps are very popular but can be expensive for home use.

A swing can be made from lengths of rope and a plank of wood and, hung from a tree, looks picturesque and will have great play value. A see-saw is easily created from a thick tree trunk, laid sideways, with a 20 cm x 10 cm long (8 in. x 4 in.) plank laid across the middle.

However, a paddling pool, preferably the moulded sort with a seat at one end, is worth buying. A bit of water play (see pages 88-9) is a good way of cooling off on a hot day.

Commercial garden equipment is excellent for summer days outside, but home-made toys are equally valuable.

Outdoor games

A party of lively children outside can be quite a proposition unless you are well prepared with ideas. One solution is to construct an obstacle course (see page 60), but there are plenty of other games which do not involve so much equipment or setting-up time.

Ball games
Young children find it very difficult to aim a ball in the right direction and catching it mid-air is even more tricky. But there are ball games that require less dexterity – and they're equally rowdy and enjoyable! Generally, use larger, softer balls for smaller children.

For *Rolling the ball* the children sit in a circle. One calls out the name of another child and rolls the ball across to them. The second child calls out another name and so on.

Pig in the middle is a rolling version of the up-in-the-air piggy game. Two children sit several feet apart and a third sits in the middle. He or she has to catch the ball as it rolls from one end to another.

In *Nose football* the ball has to be nosed from one child to another, rather than kicked. Use a large, soft ball.

Bat and ball should be played with a large, softish ball. Use old tennis rackets or other bats with a large flat surface. You throw the ball to one child at a time to hit back to you.

Rope games
Skipping (jumping rope) may or may not be appropriate for your group. Some four- and five-year-olds are excellent at it, others simply cannot manage.

Ask two older children to hold a long rope at both ends. The smaller children in turn jump over the rope:
1 as it is held still flat on the ground;
2 as it is held on the ground, but wiggled vigorously backwards and forwards to make flat waves; and
3 as the holders gently shake the rope up and down to make small vertical waves.

They may also be able to run under the rope as it is circled, and some may be able to skip over it standing still in the middle.

Even familiar party games take on an extra dimension when transferred to the great outdoors.

TUG-OF-WAR
Tug-of-war is good for a party when there are some stronger children around. Mark the ground in two places, some distance apart. Divide the children into two teams – four is the minimum number, two on each team, but the more the merrier. Each team holds one end of a long rope. The teams stand several metres or yards behind their own marks and at the signal begin to pull. The team that crosses its ground mark first loses.

Races
Wheelbarrow races are an old standby and always good fun. Pair up the children. One stands on his or her hands while a partner holds his or her legs. The first couple to cross the finishing line wins.

In *Pick-a-back races* heavier children are the packhorses, lighter ones the riders. They race to the finishing line.

Pick-a-back fights, where the riders have to bop their opponent with a very soft cushion or pillow until he or she falls off, are wonderfully exciting – but *could* end in tears.

Other ideas
We all have memories of childhood games, and generally these are fine for small children – leap frog, relay races, ring a' roses, and follow my leader for example. For some of them you have to make adaptations for small children, such as using a large ball for bat and racket games. A child's idea of tennis may not exactly resemble yours, but that doesn't make it any less enjoyable!

It's raining!

RAIN
Splat! went the rain on my nice
  clean hair
Splosh! went my feet in the
  puddle
Plop! in the mud went my old
  teddy bear
Gosh! he's a wet soggy muddle.

A splash through the puddles is great fun on a wet day – so long as you are dressed for it!

Out and about

Wet afternoons are not every parent's idea of bliss. But instead of sitting down to yet another board game and waiting until the rain stops, why not make the best use of the situation, put on waterproof clothes and wellingtons and set off for a walk? Most children don't mind the rain at all if they are properly dressed for it. Seek out puddles, walk through them, jump in them and over them, and enjoy watching the mud ooze round your boots.

If you have a pond or a lake nearby watch the raindrops hit the water and bounce off, leaving concentric circle patterns all over the surface. If there are any ducks or swans on the pond, how do they behave in the rain? One thing you can be sure of – the weather won't diminish their appetites for bits of bread. Remember to take a bag of stale bread with you!

If there are farms near you, how do cows and sheep like the rain? Where do cows seek shelter?

Look at the sky. What do clouds look like? Is the sky uniformly grey or are there huge black clouds scurrying across? Back home, ask the children to draw two kinds of skies: one for sunny weather, one for rain. What are the differences between them?

After it has stopped raining, you can go back into the garden to enjoy it. Notice how fresh it smells. Inspect flower petals and leaves and see how pretty the droplets look. Explain how plants need water to grow, and that they prefer rainwater to piped water. Can the children spot any earthworms on the surface of the soil? You should be able to see more birds than usual, attracted by the worms.

Raindrops will hang suspended from a washing line. If you lift one end carefully, the raindrops will 'slide' down to the other end before disappearing.

Catch rainwater in a container on the windowsill or in the garden. Use a plastic ruler to measure it. How many centimetres/inches fell in the night/today? Is that more than fell yesterday? (Note that rainwater is good for washing hair.)

Even town streets need not be dull. You can point out the cars zooming through puddles. What happens to pedestrians? Watch the water spread out from the wheels of the cars. See the people scurrying around with umbrellas. Those caught without umbrellas will improvise – paper bags, plastic bags, newspapers – and turn their collars up. What do the streetlamps look like when it is raining?

Indoors

Make a rainy day collage. Get the children to draw umbrellas, rubber boots, puddles, big raindrops, black clouds, and stick on appropriate materials for them – plastic bin liners, foil, buttons, felt and so on. Magazine pictures can be used too. Cut them out and stick them in a pattern on a piece of grey paper. A watery sun and a rainbow complete the picture.

Watch the raindrops cascading down a window. Do they run straight down the glass or follow a diagonal path or weave in a zigzag pattern to the bottom?

red orange yellow green blue indigo violet

RAINBOWS

A rainbow can only be seen when the sun shines through falling raindrops which then reflect the colours of the spectrum in an arc in the sky. Back home, get the children to draw one and see if they can remember the basic colours.

Windy days

You can see the sun and the rain, but you can only hear the wind and see its effects: trees bending and swaying, leaves dancing, clouds dashing across the sky, washing swinging wildly on the line, people leaning into this invisible force, wrapping their coats around them, chimneys singing as the wind swoops into the house and papers, and rubbish and umbrellas taking on a life of their own. It can be just as great for children to feel the wind on their face and in their hair as it is for you. The suggestions here will help the children understand the special properties of the wind.

How do you know it's windy?
See how many things the children come up with to judge the wind. Some will talk about the effects listed above; others will complain that the dust gets into their eyes, or that they feel cold. What about the strength of the wind, and the temperature? A warm breeze feels quite different from a freezing gale.

Which direction?
Point out smoke coming out of chimneys or from fires and flags blowing. If a child holds up a wet finger he or she can tell where the wind is coming from by the side which gets cold first. Make your own small flag-pole and put it on the windowsill or in the garden. Attach a streamer and keep an eye on it. Does the wind direction ever change?

Out and about look for weather vanes on buildings.

What will blow away?
One windy day take a selection of objects outside – a cork, pieces of aluminium foil and paper, a metal screw, a feather, some beads, sequins and a couple of soft toys. The children can hold the objects in turn on an outstretched hand to see which ones the wind moves.

Windy day collage
Make wild clouds out of cottonwool (absorbent cotton), a kite with a dangling tail of shining aluminium foil, and an umbrella and mackintoshes cut out of a black or white plastic bin liner. Use bits of fabric to make washing blowing on a clothes line (a piece of string), and more cottonwool for smoke billowing from a chimney.

WHO HAS SEEN THE WIND?
Who has seen the wind?
Neither I nor you;
But when the leaves hang
   trembling
The wind is passing through.

Who has seen the wind?
Neither you nor I;
But when the trees bow down
   their heads
The wind is passing by.

Christina Rossetti

Flying a kite is a skilful business and needs adult supervision.

What flies?

Thrilling enough indoors for small children, *a balloon* will behave in a very excited manner in the wind. Put it on a very long string, find a park and let it blow around, buffeted by gusts this way and that.

A paper dart will loop the loop in the wind. You can change its behaviour by attaching paperclips to its nose or wings.

A kite can be difficult for a child to manage, though a five-year-old should be able to hold the string once you've got it safely launched. Stand by to help.

At the water's edge

Watch the ripples on the surface of a pond or even on a puddle. They all travel one way. You can try making a paper boat, or take a toy dinghy, to sail across the pond. Ask the children how it behaves in the wind.

If you can get to the beach, where the wind and spray make walking an unusual and exciting experience, point out how the wind affects the water, sending up spray, forming white horses on top of the waves, throwing sand from the beach up on to the road and tossing boats this way and that, making it dangerous for any that are near rocky coasts.

MAKING A PARACHUTE

You'll need:
a square of tissue paper or
    plastic (from a plastic bag)
four lengths of thread about
    25 cm (10 in.) long
a little Plasticine
scissors
needle
clear sticky tape

1 Tape one end of each piece of thread to a corner of the tissue paper. Bind the other ends of the thread together with a lump of Plasticine.
2 Drop the parachute from a highish window. On a windy day it should travel some way before hitting the ground. If you make a small hole in the middle of the tissue paper with the needle, air will escape through it and the parachute will fall more steadily to the ground.

Animal tracks and trails

The best place to search for animal tracks and trails is in the country, but a large garden or a park or the grounds of a playgroup or nursery school will reveal some interesting clues to those with their noses to the ground. Foxes in Britain (and racoons and skunks in the US) are very bold and can be found in most towns, and almost any search will reveal at least bird, cat and dog prints.

Trails can be spotted and followed in dust, sand, muddy conditions or snow, so there are no seasonal limitations on this activity, although a strong wind distorts tracks in sand or snow.

Some animal signs are difficult to find, so considerable adult co-operation is essential.

In the wild

Watching wild animals requires more patience, because it's necessary to sit quietly behind a tree or in another hidden place and just wait. Dawn and dusk are the best times for spotting animals, although it is worth keeping an eye out for rabbits, squirrels and foxes (or chipmunks in the US) when walking through woodland.

Choose a spot where there are tracks or other signs which show the presence of various animals. Gnawed tree bark or pine cones with all the scales gnawed off, for instance, may show the presence of squirrels. Bits of rabbit fur caught on low branches and paired toothmarks on bark show that rabbits are in the area. The remains of an animal outside a large hole may mean a fox inside.

Look out too for broken eggshells and odd feathers on the ground. There could be an abandoned bird's nest above you worthy of inspection, but don't touch it if you find there are eggs inside. For more about birds and birdwatching, see pages 98-9.

Around your home

Keep an eye on the various domestic pets in your neighbourhood. Where do the cats walk? Where do the dogs venture? Do the birds have a favourite perch?

On a night when there is no wind, shake some flour outside your front or back door or on any piece of concreted ground or flat surface where you think animals or birds might pass. Place some bait – bits of meat, apple cores – in the middle of the floured patch.

In the morning go out with the children to see what tracks have been left behind. You may only recognize those of the old cat next door, but on the other hand you may find the footprints of some wild animal in the flour. Bird footprints are usually clearly defined. With a bit of luck there will be several lots of prints to look at. Use a book to help you identify them.

One easy trail to see outside is the snail's glossy path.

Taking casts of footprints

Animals walking on soft earth, mud or sand leave footprints behind them. Making casts of these footprints is comparatively simple and provides an excellent record for a nature table. You will have to be on hand for part of the time, however (see right).

MAKING A PLASTER CAST
You'll need:
packet of plaster of Paris (from a craft supplier)
water to mix
strips of cardboard about 2 cm (¾ in.) wide
paperclips or stapling machine

1 Clear away any dirt, leaves or twigs from around the footprint. Take some cardboard strips and encircle the footprint. Clip or staple the ends of the cardboard together.
2 Now mix up the plaster of Paris until it is a thick, sticky cream. Pour this carefully into your cardboard circle, covering the footprint completely, to a level of about 1 cm (⅜ in.).
3 When the plaster of Paris is hard (this may take up to two hours), carefully lift it from the cardboard circle. Disasters can happen at this point, so encourage the children to be gentle.

Left: *An animal's tracks can be immortalized in plaster of Paris.*

Out and about

There's a wealth of opportunities for exploration right on your own doorstep. A trip to the shops, a walk to the bus stop, a saunter round the park or over to the building site are all mini trips that provide material for the curious pre-school child.

It's a good idea for children to get to know their own area, your neighbours, their friends' families, the people who work in the shops and other familiar figures. It gives them a sense of place and belonging, widens their knowledge of other people and means that they are less likely to get themselves lost, and more likely to feel safe and protected when out and about with you.

The shops

As you go round the shops, talk about what there is to buy, and how various stores stock different goods. Ask 'What can you buy in a clothes shop?', 'Can you buy fruit and vegetables there?', 'Where would you go to buy cheese?'

Point out the till and why it is that you hand over money and the shop assistant hands some back to you. Show the children how much money you have when you start shopping and how much (or little) is left afterwards. (For more about money, see pages 42-3.)

Back home, write the words, 'clothes shop', 'bookshop', 'stationers', 'supermarket', 'hardware store', 'shoe shop' on a piece of card and see if the children would like to draw a few items that they would buy in those shops. Or put a selection of such items on a table. When you call out the name of a shop, the children have to bring you something you would purchase there.

The post office

Stamps, parcels and airmail letters, can all be the starting point for stories explaining the workings of the post office.

Address letters to your children or a favourite pet, perhaps containing a drawing, and let him or her put a stamp on it and post it. See how long it is before it arrives at home.

Get the children to design their own stamps for writing letters to friends or members of the family. They must deliver them by hand; explain why. If you receive letters from abroad, the children may want to collect the stamps.

ROAD SAFETY

Instil road sense in your children from the earliest age. Always stop at the kerb and go through a crossing drill with them. Make sure they look each way two or three times, and listen hard for vehicles which might not be in view but coming round the corner. Remind them never to cross between parked cars, or to chase a ball into the road. Practise the drill until it becomes second nature.

The bank

All children seem irresistibly drawn towards bank stationery. They love drawing on it, seeming desperate to make an early mark on the financial world. Otherwise, though, banking money is a difficult concept.

Show them the procedure for writing cheques and collecting cash from the teller, explaining that it is not the bank's money that you are being given, but your own that they are keeping safe.

Environmental print

There's no reason why you can't make use of signposts, road names, advertisements, petrol station signs and other environmental print to help the older pre-school child approach reading (see pages 54-7). The slick rhymes of advertisements, linked as they often are with television programmes, stick easily in the memory, and they'll come to recognize the words on hoardings when pointed out and then be able to spot them when they crop up in books.

Other things you see written up in print – 'Danger – Beware', 'Keep left', 'No right turn', 'School', 'Hospital', 'Children crossing' – can also be pointed out to the children. They'll soon be calling out the words themselves.

Helping with the shopping is an educational experience. How many carrots make a pound?

All about trees

Trees stretch a long way above the heads of small children, so it's hardly surprising that they are far less likely to be aware of different sorts of trees than they are of flowers which they can bend down to and compare quite easily.

Apart from their own special properties, trees harbour a magic wonderland of life. At any time of the year they are a whole world to explore and delight in.

Identifying trees

Buy a book with good-quality colour pictures of common trees, their leaves and seeds. The children will enjoy looking at the pictures and comparing them with the real thing in the park or countryside.

There are two main kinds of trees, evergreens and deciduous. Evergreens do not keep the same leaves all the time, as some children think, but are continuously shedding and regrowing their greenery. That is why they always look green, even in winter. Deciduous trees shed their leaves in late autumn, leaving bare branches. They grow new leaves in the spring of each year. It will be up to you to point out that each variety of tree has different bark, is taller or smaller, fatter or thinner, and has different shaped leaves.

Collect some leaves of evergreen and deciduous trees and press them like flowers between sheets of absorbent paper in a heavy book (see flower pressing, pages 86-7). When they have dried out they can be mounted on card and labelled.

Tree structure

It's difficult to see the roots of a tree, though sometimes in a wood you can see them stretching out a long way from the tree trunk. Get the children to find the root which lies furthest away.

If a tree is uprooted in a storm and lying on its side, you'll have a good opportunity to point out the root system. Explain that trees take in water through their roots in the same way as smaller plants.

The bark of a tree can be smooth, as on a beech tree, flaking, where patches of bark break away as the tree ages, as on sycamore or horse chestnut, or peeling, in which strips break away horizontally as they grow older, as on a birch tree. The bark is a protective covering. The tree grows beneath it, channelling sap from the roots up to the leaves.

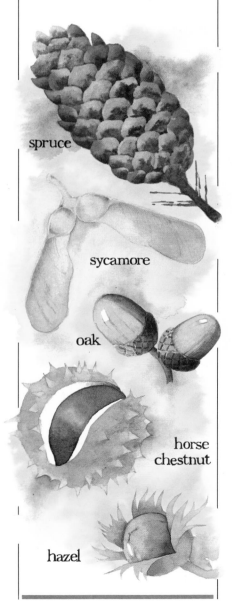

SEEDS
All trees have their own seeds, and some are very distinctive. Look for the cones of pine trees, spruce, larch, hemlock, cedar – they are all different.

Many seeds bear hairs or wings so that the wind can carry them. Look for the seeds of alders, birches, elms, larches. Use a book to identify them.

spruce

sycamore

oak

horse chestnut

hazel

Left: *It's amazing just how much life you can find in the bark of a tree, and a blackberrying expedition* (above) *will reveal a host of interesting creatures as well as the ingredients for a delicious pie.*

Tree life

The bark of a tree is a home for all kinds of tiny animals and plants. These can be examined on the tree with the naked eye but you will see more with a magnifying glass. Do not strip off pieces of bark for the purpose, as it damages the trees.

Birds, of course, nest in trees. Let the children watch how they come and go, note their singing and see if they can see bird nests. If you do find a nest, be careful not to disturb, or even touch, the eggs, as if you do, the mother bird will reject the eggs. (For more about birdwatching, see pages 98-9.)

In woodland, squirrels, mice and voles scamper around the trees collecting nuts and seeds for their hoards. And under the leaf mould lying on the ground, your children will find a whole new world of woodlice, slugs and snails, mites, earthworms, caterpillars and other creatures worth inspection.

Trees need conservation. It's quite possible to plant a small woodland tree in your own garden. But take advice from a good garden centre or, in Britain, The Woodland Trust (see page 117 for address), in the US, your state's Extension Service.

Trips out

All trips out need careful planning and preparation – just enough for the children to understand where they are going and why and what kinds of things they are likely to see. Anticipation and discussion are all part of the fun, but don't make too much of the occasion in advance, just in case something goes wrong and you can't go.

Museums, art galleries, the local fire station or zoo are all good trips for young children, as, depending on where you live, is a visit to the airport, but do try to make sure the excursion isn't too long. Better to have the children beg to stay an extra five minutes than to have them ask 'Can we go home now?'

A visit to the zoo is a great outing on a summer's day.

Museum and art gallery

Choose museums that cater especially for children, or those that feature something that already interests your children, such as railway engines. Many museums have working models you can operate with a push-button. Research these in your area, or look in the local press.

Some establishments now produce leaflets and activity books for children. Try to pick up these in advance of the trip, so that you can talk through the exhibits and have preliminary discussions about the Romans, the Red Indians or whatever.

With art galleries, be very selective in what you see. Again, try to pick up catalogues and special children's publications in advance, or at least buy these when you get there and look through them over a snack. Decide how much you are going to see and stick to it, concentrating on works you know will have something to interest your child. Contrary to what you may fear, three- and four-year-olds are not bored by paintings, but half an hour is usually enough.

Zoo

Do not try to see everything. It's tempting to plod round doggedly because, after all, you don't get there very often and it's expensive, but a whole day walking round is counter-productive.

Be guided by what your children would like to see, add one or two more interesting or exotic animals that you think they'd like, then opt for an ice-cream and home. This way you'll be able to spend more time with each animal and learn about its eating, sleeping, swimming and grooming habits without feeling under pressure to get on.

Rivers and canals

It should be possible to take some kind of trip on a river or canal – on a narrow boat, or a pleasure cruiser or in a rowing boat. Explain that some rivers and most canals are like roads and are used to transport goods from one place to another. A canal with locks to negotiate offers an interesting trip. Ducks, swans, fish, frogs and other freshwater creatures can also be spotted, perhaps with the help of binoculars. Waterfalls, weirs and stepping stones are all very exciting spots for a river picnic, but keep a firm grip on small hands.

If you live near a port or harbour, a trip to see the different boats, their passengers and cargo, perhaps some fish being landed, is also an interesting experience.

After the trip

Chat about the outing when you get home. What did the children like best? What didn't they like? What special smells and sights do they remember?

Encourage drawings of the trip. If you have taken several children, let them do a group picture, deciding themselves which part of it they want to do. A picture diary is a good idea; use illustrations cut from old magazines.

Relive the trip through a dramatization of the day's events. The children dictate the story and then act it out.

FIRE STATION

Some fire stations have an open day when children can go round, climb on the engines, stroke the shining livery and experience close-up the drama of these big red engines.

If your fire station does not have an open day, ring and ask when it would be convenient to make a visit. Take several children.

At the pond

Whether you live in the town or country, there'll be a pond somewhere near you. And wherever there's a pond, however unappealing it may look to you, there's life. A pond is a ready-made science laboratory, filled with creatures normally hidden away from view carrying on their lives without much help from us.

Arm the family or group with screw-top jars, with holes punched in the lids, and fishing-nets, and set off to investigate.

Algae

Wherever rainwater collects and stays for a while, algae will grow. Demonstrate this if you have a garden and no pond by digging a hole in a flowerbed when the weather is wet and sinking a large flowerpot. Leave it there to collect rainwater naturally and see what happens. After a week or so a green slime will form on top of the water. This is called algae. Find a pond, pull aside the green slimy algae and see what you can find.

Surface creatures

Pond skaters and water measurers are very plentiful and are probably the first animals you'll come across. Water measurers – wingless insects with a long odd shape, and eyes set a long way down their bodies – are very light, with a hairy coat, and can walk very slowly on the pondwater without breaking the surface film of the water.

Pond skaters travel much more quickly over the water and sometimes jump a long way. Some have wings and some don't. They also have a thick coat of hairs which holds air and helps keep them dry. Neither pond skaters nor water measurers can live under the water.

Whirligig beetles whizz round and round over the surface of the water. Their legs are wide and flat to help them swim really fast. They also have specially adapted eyes to allow them to see above and below the surface of the water and keep an eye out for enemies.

Water-lilies

Water-lilies have long leaf-stalks and very heavy leaves which are supported by the water. The seeds disperse by floating away from the fully grown water-lily in a mass of air bubbles. The bubbles burst and the seeds sink to the bottom of the ground to grow into new plants.

Safety notes
Even harmless-looking garden ponds can be dangerous for a small child, and indeed such a pond should be covered with boards unless you are in the garden to keep an eye on things. Keep an eye on children near any pond and do not let them approach the edge unless you are within arm's distance.

A net is essential for collecting plants and animals from the pond.

Frogs, toads and newts

In the spring you may see frogspawn sitting like spotted jelly on top of the water. Toad spawn is usually attached or wound round pondweed in a long, transparent worm. Newt larvae should be around in the spring and summer. They look a bit like tadpoles, except that they have thinner bodies and longer tails.

Dragonflies

Watch out for these because they are so beautiful and children love tracing them as they hover and dart over the surface of the pond, their wings catching the light and glistening in the sun. A dragonfly takes several hours to emerge from its larval skin, so you could well catch the rather aggressive larva, enemy of many tiny underwater creatures, turning into a delicate and lovely creature.

Larger animals

Look out for water voles and shrews, which live on the banks of larger ponds and will drop with a splash into the water when you approach. Mallards can often be seen sharing the water with other water fowl.

Use the nets and screw-top jars (filled with pondwater) to collect a few other animals and plants the children find and take them back home for identification. A microscope, of course, is a great asset, but much can be learned without one. Return all specimens to their natural habitat within a couple of days.

Conservation note
Never remove frog, toad or newt spawn from ponds – stocks are easily depleted. It is now illegal in the UK to remove the spawn of the great-crested newt.

How things grow

Soil feels wonderful between the fingers, and there's so much you can do with it. Not only can it be poked, patted, dug up, smoothed down and made into pies, it even makes things grow!

If you have no garden, windowboxes and patio tubs are perfect receptacles for all kinds of lovely flowers and herbs and even the smallest flowerpot contains an extraordinary number of small miracles.

Light, water and warmth

Explain to the children that plants take water from the soil and that in the water are important nutrients which the plant manufactures into food with the aid of sunlight. The sap of the plant carries the water and nutrients to the leaves which is where the process takes place.

What happens if you don't water plants? Demonstrate by letting a quickly responsive plant such as a Busy Lizzie *(impatiens)* go without water for a bit too long. The leaves droop dramatically. Water it and it will perk up within an hour or two.

Seeds

Choose some hardy annual seeds that can be planted in spring. Nasturtiums, forget-me-nots, zinnias and marigolds can all be sown outdoors in late spring and look lovely in a sunny corner of the garden. Watch them push up through the soil, grow tall and strong stems, and finally flowers. Check each seed packet for sowing instructions and the best type of soil for each variety.

Explain about pollination. Bees, intent on collecting nectar for making honey, are attracted to the colourful, scented flowers, and in extracting the nectar pick up pollen from the stamens on their legs. Any garden on a mild day will soon produce examples. Explain how when the bees go to another flower they deposit the pollen on the stigma; this eventually grows into a new seed ready to be planted.

Bulbs

Anemones, scilla, crocus, daffodil, narcissus, snowdrop and tulip are good hardy bulbs that children can grow quite easily either in a windowbox or in their own garden patch (as long as you live somewhere with a suitable climate). They are easier to clutch in a small hand than seeds and make equally satisfying progress.

SUNFLOWERS

Sunflowers deserve a special mention because they grow at such an exciting rate and look so wonderfully dramatic when they're fully grown. The seed heads are well worth a close inspection. Sunflower seeds taste good in salads and hamsters love them!

The bulbs will need watering, of course, especially as the weather gets warmer and the soil drier. Put the children in charge of watering (work out a rota if necessary) and provide them with a light watering can.

If you can lay your hands on the kind of brick which has a grid of holes, put this on a quarry tile, fill each hole with potting compost and plant it with snowdrops and crocus corms. Put it outside the children's bedroom window so they can watch the flowers spring up in the brick.

Herb windowboxes

A very convenient way to grow herbs is right outside a sunny kitchen window. They need sunshine and a light, fertile soil, so fill the windowbox with compost. Plant seeds (dill and coriander grow quickly) or small plants bought at nurseries or garden centres.

Also available are little peat pots containing seeds of one kind of herb and a suitable soil. You just moisten the pots and place them on a sunny windowsill. When they start to grow they can be planted, still in their pots in a larger clay pot filled with soil.

Keeping a growing chart

Weekly drawings of the progress of seeds and bulbs in your children's windowbox or garden, along with a note of how much water they've been given and how much sunshine they've had in that time, keep up interest and provide a useful record for small gardeners.

It needs patience and care, but the magic results of planting make all that effort worth while.

Visiting a farm

A trip to a farm at any time of the year is interesting, but in spring there are lambs and calves to look at, and if you're lucky, ducklings or chicks too.

Some cities now operate small farms so that children in built-up areas can get some idea of what happens on the large-scale version. Try to visit one of these if you can't get out to the country. It is, of course, essential to phone a commercial farmer to ask if you can visit, explaining how many adults and children would like to come.

Many farms offer family holidays or weekends. These really are a treat for young children who are often allowed to help with the milking, collect the eggs or muck in with other chores around the farmhouse and in the fields. They may also be able to ride ponies and give a hand in the stables. Some lambs have to be hand-reared and will follow a child allowed to feed them with a bottle, which is very thrilling. Good home cooking is usually part of a farm-holiday deal, so it's likely to be very enjoyable for all the family.

Preparing for the trip

Look together at simple books on farm animals, crops and farm machinery, and talk about the different types of farm: fruit farms, dairy farms, pig farms, cereal crops and so on. On a practical note, insect repellent and sting remedies may be useful, a change of clothes could be welcome, and waterproof boots are a must.

Animals

Cows, sheep, chickens, ducks, horses, pigs, goats, geese and donkeys are all kept on farms. Explain that farm animals are not pets (a common misunderstanding) but are reared either for what they can produce – eggs, milk, wool, down or fur – or for their meat. Meat-producing animals are reared on the farm, sold at market and killed. Some children – and adults – find this a very unpleasant fact but it is interesting to explain the connection between the frozen chicken trussed up in the supermarket, for example, and that very lively, messy animal strutting around the farmyard. (Of course, most of the chickens we eat are reared in 'battery' farms. These are not pleasant places for children to visit, and are upsetting for even the most enthusiastic adult meat-eaters.)

A model farm with toy animals, cattle sheds, sheep pens and fields of

Safety notes

Farms are dangerous places for children. It's not only the working machinery that's deadly, but also the occasional rusty spade or fork lying forgotten and half hidden in the long grass. Young children need to be kept under strict supervision and reminded not to frighten the animals. Do remember too always to shut gates behind you when you are walking around a farm or through fields. And watch out for nettle-beds: a tumble in nettles can ruin a day's outing.

Why are some eggs brown and some white? Be prepared for some searching questions down on the farm!

crops is a useful toy. It can be made or bought cheaply and extended with paper stuck to board (for fields). Talk through the process of milking the cows, letting the children move the cows from the fields into the milking parlour; and explain how sheep are rounded up for dipping or shearing by sheep-dogs. Toy 'eggs' (tiny balls of aluminium foil) can be collected from the hens, and ducks settled on a pond (more aluminium foil or a round pocket mirror).

Machines
Toy tractors and combine harvesters are good educational toys and can be incorporated in the toy farm. Explain that tractors pull ploughs and other heavy machinery, and that combine harvesters are used to reap and thresh cereal crops (that is, cut the crops and separate out the grain).

Crops
Explain that bread is made from wheat grown on farms, and that other cereals such as barley and all kind of fruit and vegetables are grown on different kinds of farm. In spring the trees on fruit farms will be full of blossom. If you can make another visit in late summer to see the ripe fruit take the place of blossom, so much the better.

FARM GAMES
Traditional songs such as 'The Farmer's in his Den' and 'Old Macdonald' are favourites with many children. Help the children cut out pictures of lots of different animals and machinery (machines make noises too!) and use them as props for 'Old Macdonald'.

A group of several children can be divided into sheep, goats, cattle or geese. You'll need volunteers for the farmer, sheep-dog and farmhands to round up the animals, milk, shear, plant crops, rake in the hay for animal feed and so on. Encourage conversation about the health of the animals, suitable weather for harvesting, the amount of milk being collected or anything else you have found in books or chatted about that may provide a talking point. You'll soon have a real working farm in your kitchen or garden!

Plants from scraps

There's nothing quite like planting a small seed and seeing it sprout magnificent foliage for convincing even the most sceptical person that nature really is something special. And the great thing is that all kinds of domestic 'rubbish' will get results. Orange pips, avocado stones, date stones, and carrot tops can all be used to create a splendid indoor garden.

You'll need some saucers, jam-jars (jelly glasses), seed mixture, 12 cm (5 in.) flowerpots, some proprietary compost and a little patience. For the plants, take your pick from the ideas below.

Recording progress
Ask the children to describe what they're doing at each stage, and what happens to the plants. Keep a diary if they seem interested – they might like to illustrate it – and suggest that they keep a 'growth chart' and a 'watering and care rota' so that the new plants are not neglected.

Carrots, parsnips, turnips and beetroot
All these very ordinary vegetables produce pretty, ferny plants without soil. Cut the top 2 cm (1 in.) or so from as many large, fresh vegetables as you have children. The embryo plants can be stood in saucers of water on a well-lit windowsill. Make sure the water in the saucers is kept topped up and the vegetables will soon sprout.

Pineapple plants
More exotic than potatoes are pineapple plants. Some, however, refuse to take root, and others go mouldy, so although pineapples can be expensive, to avoid disappointment it's a good idea to try to grow two or three, or other things, at the same time. Make sure the fruit is fresh, cut off the top including 2 cm (1 in.) of fruit, then cut round leaving a cork-shaped lump underneath the sprouting top. Hang in a dry, warm place until the flesh is dry.

Now get the children to remove the bottom leaves and plant in a damp, sandy potting mix. The pot needs to be kept in a light, warm place – at least 18° C (64° F) at night. Spray with water regularly, but do not keep the potting mixture too wet. Once it has taken root, water and feed the plant regularly. (It *might* produce fruit, but if it does it's going to take a few years, so it won't be seen in the pre-school years.)

Safety notes
You'll need sharp knives for cutting the tops off root vegetables or a pineapple, so keep these away from the children and do this work for them.

82

Ginger and coffee

Ginger roots have to be suspended in water until they sprout, and then planted in potting mixture. If you keep the plants warm and light, they should soon produce exciting-looking plants.

Fresh, unroasted coffee beans need warm, damp potting mixture to germinate, and once they have started to sprout they prefer warm conditions – 10° C (50° F) – and thrive in a shady, airy place. The first coppery leaves turn a glossy dark green and the sweet-smelling white flowers are eventually replaced by red berries containing coffee beans.

Melon or pumpkin seeds

These should be collected and dried in the sun, sown in seed mixture and kept warm. They can then be transferred to pots and trained up poles or around window frames.

Beans, lentils and peas

These are all excellent standbys for explaining to children how seeds sprout. Put a few mixed seeds between some damp blotting paper and the sides of jam-jars, about halfway up the jars to allow the shoots and roots space to grow. A little warm water in the jars will ensure that the blotting paper stays wet. Keep the jars in a warm place. Progress is quick and satisfying.

POTATOES

You'll need seed potatoes with plenty of eyes, and a jam-jar for each one.

1 Let each child choose a potato to fit his or her jam-jar snugly, eyes turned upwards. (Some smaller ones may need to be suspended from long pins or cocktail sticks resting on the edges of the jam-jars.)
2 Fill the jars with water so that the potatoes just rest in the water.
3 The jars need to be kept in a dark, cool place until the potatoes grow roots and start to sprout. Then they can be planted in potting compost. All but one or two shoots should be cut off. The potatoes will grow into trailing plants that can be draped round the children's bedroom window frame.

Carrots, parsnips, and potatoes all produce interesting-looking plants in only a few weeks.

Off for a picnic

Why it is that eating out of doors should be so thrilling is quite a mystery, but thrilling it is, and setting off into the country on a picnic is downright adventurous – you just never know what might happen. That's certainly how children view the prospect, even if your approach is more practical.

Involve the children as much as possible in the preparation, not just of the food, but of the complete picnic – from where you are going to go, to cutlery, games to play and rubbish bags. Of course, they will need help or it will be a chore, but they will enjoy a degree of responsibility in helping you foresee every eventuality.

Let them help you make a list of everything you might need and get them to lay out the picnic plates, knives and forks, making sure they have a set for everyone coming. Remember a wet cloth for dirty faces and hands, kitchen rolls for spills, drinks, unbreakable cups, a special cup for the baby, hot drinks, tissues, 'something to do' – an activity book, crayons and paper, for instance, or any favourite toys. Try to get the children to think for themselves what each member of the family or group might need.

Recipes for success

Tempting food for the occasion is obviously first on the list. Here are one or two variations on the ordinary sandwich which four- and five-year-olds can help prepare, and other good picnic food which the children will enjoy.

Sandwich shapes are easier to make if you use sliced bread. The children fill the sandwiches as usual, with something not too squashy, such as peanut butter, cheese, or ham and chives, then use biscuit (cookie) cutters to press out hearts, circles, squares, diamonds. For once, discard the crusts.

Pitta bread cut in half and opened out into pockets make ideal picnic containers. Fill them with a chicken, sweetcorn and mayonnaise mix or any other favourite filling and wrap them in aluminium foil.

Other goodies to take include chicken drumsticks (the children can roll the raw chicken in egg and breadcrumbs before they are cooked), spare ribs, and salads your helpers can help mix and dress.

Fresh fruit salad in a plastic box is also good picnic food. This can involve several children in the preparation. They won't be able to peel and core the apples (but can probably chop them with your supervision), but they can dissect oranges you've already peeled, cut up a banana or two, take the pips out of grapes, stir the mixture up and pour on a couple of cups of fresh or cartoned orange or pineapple juice.

Spotting wildlife

If you rarely get a chance to spend a day in the country, make the most of it. Take books to help you identify species of wild flowers, trees, birds and other creatures and spend a little time looking carefully into hedgerows or investigating ponds (see pages 86-7 and 76-7).

MAKING NEAPOLITAN SANDWICHES

You'll need:
1 unsliced white loaf
1 unsliced wholemeal
   or wholewheat loaf
polyunsaturated margarine
2 or 3 different fillings

1 Cut the loaves into long, horizontal slices. Get one child to spread each slice with margarine, while you, or another child, add the fillings in turn on to alternate white and brown slices.
2 Pile the slices on top of one another, ending with a slice of bread without margarine or filling.
3 Wrap the loaves in aluminium foil or clingfilm (plastic wrap) and chill in the refrigerator.
4 Cut vertically at the picnic site (with a good serrated knife) and you'll have a very sophisticated and colourful pile of sandwiches.

At last it's time to eat the goodies! A picnic gives children a chance to work together.

Wild flowers

Wild flowers are a miracle, particularly for those of us who beaver away in the garden with little to show for it, and for children who rarely get to see flowers. Inspecting and admiring them provide an excellent motivation for a summer's walk.

It is important to remember that flowers produce fruit, which contain seeds. When the fruit is ripe, the seeds are dispersed and produce more flowers. If wild flowers are picked, there will be no seeds, and no more flowers. It is, in fact, illegal to pick many wild flowers, and the best thing is therefore not to pick any at all. *You* may understand the rules, but it is unlikely that children will learn to distinguish between the different flowers and conditions. If you find rare flowers, keep the fact to yourself so that the stock is not depleted by irresponsible people.

Pressing a collection gives you an extra opportunity to look closely at the parts of a flower together.

Looking at flowers

Buy a good wild flower book to help you identify the plants. You will need to look carefully at the colour, leaf shape, flower shape and colour, the number and arrangement of the sepals, petals, stamens and carpels. For some of the tinier flowers you will need a magnifying glass.

Sit down with the children and look at the flowers together. Point out the different parts, note the number and texture of the leaves, the petals and the stamens. Is there any pollen?

Pressing garden flowers

Pressing flowers captures a special moment, and brings back the memory of a perfect summer's day. The flattened plant looks quite different from the original, yet is so obviously the same. It can be inspected all over again.

Commercial flower presses are cheap and work well, but they're not necessary. Blotting paper or paper tissues and a heavy book or two will do just as well. Lay the flower on one sheet of blotting paper, cover it with another, shut the book, put another book on top and leave the flowers undisturbed for four or five weeks. They can then be moved if you like and will survive without blotting paper if handled carefully. But they are delicate.

Smaller flowers with less fleshy petals are best, though of course rose petals can be pressed separately. It's lovely to open a favourite book and find a flower to remind you of a particular occasion.

Pressed flower collage

Well pressed flowers can be used to make attractive cards. Use either whole flowers, or make patterns with the petals of various flowers.

Help the children to choose colours to tone in carefully, then cover the card with a commercial transparent seal. For a change use black paper for the backing. Pressed flower pictures look very pretty framed.

A good idea is to collect a specimen of all the types of flowers growing in your neighbourhood, and help the children press them and make a labelled wallchart.

Drying flowers

Many flowers can be preserved simply by hanging them up to dry in an airy place. Strip the leaves off first and then tie a few together at the stem and hang the bunch upside-down.

Sand can also be used. You'll need silver sand, available from nurseries. Simply fill a box, tie wire around the stems of the flowers and place the flowers in the box, covering them completely with sand. The flowers will dry in four weeks or so.

Glycerine drying is most suitable for large bunches of leaves. Mix one part glycerine to three parts warm water and put into a jar. Split the branches with a knife up the stem and stand them in the solution, which you may have to top up. When the leaves begin to darken, remove them and hang upside-down in a dark, warm cupboard to dry out.

Ask for the children's help throughout. They'll learn a lot about flowers from handling them at every stage.

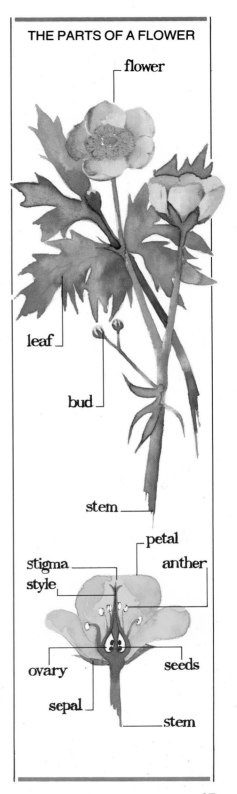

THE PARTS OF A FLOWER

flower

leaf

bud

stem

stigma

style

petal

anther

ovary

seeds

sepal

stem

Fun with water

Water sparkles, drips, splashes, plops and makes a wonderful mess. Let the children play on their own with an old teapot, plastic cups, a ladle, saucepans, a funnel, sieve, tea strainer – anything that will help them discover the properties of water.

Don't give them too much equipment at a time or they're likely to get tired and confused. Playing with water outside solves a lot of mess problems and allows the children much more freedom, though of course most of these activities can take place in the kitchen too.

The bubble bowl

Bubbles are quite magical, floating on air, gleaming with colour, changing shape, sticking together, dividing and falling – all to screeches of glee. Supply a bowl of lukewarm water, plenty of washing-up liquid and plastic rings of various sizes. Point out the colours in the bubbles. How far do the bubbles travel before they burst? What happens if they are blown gently? Very hard? Can you catch them?

Ice cubes

Take a bowl of ice cubes out into the garden and let the children experiment, dropping them into warm and cold water to see how they crack or melt. Suggest they pour a stream of water on to an ice cube and watch a hole appear (this works well in the sink with the cold tap on full).

Oil slicks

Bath oil, cooking oil, and oil paints all make interesting patterns when dripped on to the surface of a bowl of water and swirled around with fingertips or a stick (paints floated in water in this way can be used for marbling paper, see page 17).

Take the opportunity to explain that oil, grease and wax repel water. Hands smeared with hand cream, margarine or oil will not get wet when dipped in cold water. Washing-up liquid and suds, on the other hand, dissolve grease. Demonstrate by letting the children wash up some greasy plates.

Draw a candle over a piece of card and pour on some water. The unwaxed areas will soak up the liquid, the waxed areas will stay dry. Explain why this is so.

Safety notes

Don't leave young children on their own with a container of water which they could fall into: they can drown in a very small amount. Make sure there are no sharp knives hiding under the washing-up suds. Some children are allergic to bubble bath, bath oil etc. so it's best to stick to reputable varieties produced for babies.

Plenty for everyone! Let loose with water and some simple equipment, children will learn a good deal about the properties of this excellent play material.

Floating and sinking

Select a number of different objects, some that float and some that sink. Let the children discover for themselves which does what. Afterwards they could make a simple chart by drawing the objects in the appropriate 'float' and 'sink' columns. Help them make paper boats which they can colour and sail in the bath.

Which holds more?

Take two different-shaped containers and fill each with the same amount of water. Does one look more full than the other? The point is that water has no shape of its own, but always takes the shape of its container. The children can pour the water from one container to another and then experiment with other cups, jugs and bowls.

Water play is one of the best entertainment standbys for all ages. Don't forget to use bathtime for some extra activities.

89

At the beach

The water's edge holds all kinds of treasures to be collected, sorted, identified and admired.

A day at the beach is not only a family treat. With sand and water to play with, animals to inspect and shells to admire, it's also a real education. So if you're within reach of the coast, next time the sun makes a watery appearance head for the beach!

Sand

Sand has a fine, grainy texture and flows rather like water between fingers and toes. And it's great for jumping and rolling on, digging in and generally providing an extra special playground. Building sandcastles and 'digging down to water' are favourite activities, and demonstrate the different properties of wet and dry sand. While they're playing, get the children to keep an eye out for signs of life. (See pages 92-3 for more sand play ideas.)

Burrowing animals

Lugworm casts are the easily spotted, spiral-shaped 'houses' seen on damp sand when the tide is out.

Sand-hoppers are helpful creatures as they eat decaying seaweed and dead crabs. They 'hop' by pushing against the ground with their tails and then quickly straightening out their bodies.

Razor-shells, cockles, sandgapers and clams live under the sand and poke two tubes out to the surface, one to bring in food and water and the other to pump out water and waste products.

Sand-eels like digging themselves into fine sand using their very efficient, long jaws. The sand hides the eel from birds and large fish.

Eel-grass feeds all kinds of animals that live around its long stems or under the sand near its roots.

The rock pool

Rock pools are full of animals and plants which can vary depending on how far up the beach they are. You will usually be able to see members of the mollusc family (which includes limpets, mussels and dogwhelks) and the crab family (these are crustaceans, related to insects and spiders). Common shore crabs are plentiful on the lower parts of many beaches, and you may also see hermit crabs and edible crabs.

Safety notes

Even the safest beaches hold dangers. Children can disappear behind sand dunes, fall into tidal pools, wander off into the surf to find a special treasure, clamber over sharp rocks, broken glass or old cans and cut their feet. So make sure they stick by an adult and are properly dressed for the outing. A portable first-aid kit, including cream for insect bites, is a must.

SHELLS

Suggest that the children collect as many different kinds of shells as they can. These are very useful for collages or for sticking on to boxes to make unusual gifts. They will also look good on a nature table at home or at playgroup. Special shells can be varnished to give them a permanent shine. But make sure that they are thoroughly cleaned and scrubbed before being stuck on to some craftwork, or someone may get a rather smelly present!

dog whelk

scallop

mussel

tower

razor

Seaweed

See if the children can find:

Bladder wrack, the common, leathery, brown seaweed found on the middle shore.

Thong weed, greeny-brown plants which are found on the lower shore and have offshoots growing from the top of each plant.

Irish moss, which is found on the middle and lower parts of rocky shores and varies in colour from green or pink to a dark reddish-brown.

A collection of dried seaweed makes an interesting arrangement for a windowsill in a child's room.

Playing with sand

Children need little coaxing to dig into a sand tray in the garden. Sand is such a versatile material; it's perfect for pies, castles, little dishes, tunnels, and for experiments in pouring, measuring, and burying treasures. When it's dry, it's clean and pure, and when wet, sticky and messy. It's altogether very satisfactory stuff for playtime, as sand and children are a great mixture.

What to provide

The beach, of course, is free, but if you're relying on the back yard or garden you'll need a large deep tray of some kind, preferably two – one for dry sand and one for wet. Drawers from an old chest are fine. You can put these on the ground, though it's easier for children to get at if they're set on a table top.

Buy silver sand from educational suppliers, because builders' sand doesn't pour very well and is dirty and sticky.

Keep buckets, funnels, spades and other equipment by, but don't forget to encourage the children to experience the properties of sand with their fingers and hands. They'll soon discover the differences between wet and dry sand. Dry sand runs through their fingers, falls from their hands into a mountain peak, fills holes, obliterates drawings and squiggles, fills cups and buckets, and hides their toys. Wet sand can be used to build elaborate structures worthy of great architects. A group of children may well collaborate over a particular venture – all good practice in co-operation and give and take, though unlikely to be argument-free.

Cooking games

It's unlikely that you'll need to suggest much, but if invention flags, wet sand, festooned with pebbles or sticks can be fashioned into delicious meals and snacks. It's an opportunity to explain the ingredients needed for a cake. Bits of sand or pebbles can represent the butter, sugar, flour and flavouring, and a little box makes a perfectly adequate oven.

Sand bag dolls

Sew together a couple of pieces of fabric into a frog shape or a doll (use close stitches), and fill about two-thirds full with sand. Stitch on eyes, ears, and so on, and you have a surprisingly flexible toy.

Safety notes
There's something irresistible about throwing sand around. As it can get in other children's faces and cause very sore eyes and tears, it's an activity that must be discouraged. If you keep your sand trays outside, cover them when not in use to protect them from animals and rain. Also, sand is not going to be much good for the insides of your washing machine, so shake sandy clothes well prior to washing.

Punch bags

Small boxers will enjoy letting off steam by attacking a sand bag. Fill up a shoebag with sand and hang it from a tree. Do not make the string too long or the bag will swing too far. A set of boxing gloves (mittens will do) and a pair of shorts complete the picture.

Sand casts

This is fun if you have a large sandpit available or if you're planning a trip to the beach. You'll need slightly damp sand which is not too hard. Get the children to lie down in the sand, and – gently – press their bodies into it, not forgetting their hands, heels and head. When they stand up carefully, their impression should be left on the ground. They can then fill in their features with sticks, pebbles and shells. You can create 'casts' of the entire family and watch them get swallowed up by the tide.

Sand is perfect for making mud pies, cakes, tunnels – and just as good to squeeze through your fingers and pat down hard.

Keeping insects and garden animals

They may be creepie-crawlies to you and Grandma, but if you can bear it, keeping insects is easy, cheap, enjoyable for children and very educational. And if you don't know how worms live, or what a stick insect looks like, or how much food an ant can carry at a time, you'll find keeping these creatures as interesting as the children do. Encourage the children to keep a record of the lives of their insects.

Safety notes
None of these insects or animals are harmful, though children could harm them if rough or clumsy.

Ant colony
You'll need a large jar, bowl or tank, soil or sand, muslin to cover the container, an elastic band (elastic) or string, a larger bowl or tray filled with water, and a cloth to cover the ant colony.

Ants are great fun. They live in organized, efficient settlements, and are very hard workers. They are blind, relying on their other senses to find their way around and build their great cities inhabited by a rigid structure of workers, soldiers and the queen ant who, having mated, does nothing but lay eggs.

Help the children get the ants' home ready first. Your large jar or tank should be one-third filled with light soil or sand, and you should stand this in a larger bowl of water. This means that if the ants do escape from the jar at least they won't take over the house.

Look for an ants' nest in the garden or park, in the ground, in roots and in rotted wood. Collect a good number in the jar, scooping up as much of the nest as possible, earth and all. Check for the queen. She is bigger and will be surrounded by winged drones (males). Also make sure you collect some eggs (little white specks) and pupae, so that you have a complete ant colony.

You'll need to clamp the muslin over the top of the jar quickly to prevent the ants escaping. Cover them with a large cloth and leave them to settle down. Don't let the earth get too dry or the ants will die (spray it with water) and remember not to leave the ant colony in a bright light. The ants will need to be fed on small earthworms, dead beetles or flies, meat scraps and sugar.

Stick insects
You'll need a large jar or goldfish bowl, muslin, sand or soil for the bottom of the jar, a small jar of water to fit inside the large jar, and cottonwool (absorbent cotton).

Stick insects are very odd-looking – as you might expect, just like twigs. They can be found in privet hedges or bought from pet shops. They need a good supply of privet leaves to eat, fresh ones every day.

Line the bottom of a large jar with sand or soil, and set in this a smaller jar containing water for the privet branch. Plug the hole with cottonwool or tissues to stop your insects drowning. Put the insects into the jar, and cover the top with muslin.

Female stick insects are bigger than males and lay eggs without being fertilized. So if you own a female you'll probably end up with a whole family of stick insects.

Worms

You'll need a large jam-jar (jelly glass), sand and soil, a dark cloth, some muslin, and leaves for food.

Collect one or two worms by digging up a patch of flowerbed or watering the lawn to bring them to the surface.

Fill your jar with alternate layers of damp sand and soil. Put a few leaves on top and wrap a dark cloth around the sides of the jar (so that the worms will burrow away around the edge of the glass and not be put off by the light). Pop the worms on top and secure the jar with muslin. Leave them for a day or two and then take off the wrapping so that the children can see the patterns made by the wriggling, stretching, burrowing worms. They might like to draw a picture of the result.

Stick insects can be kept in an old aquarium instead of a jar. The top will need to be covered with muslin.

Snow and ice

Crunchy underfoot, freezing on the fingers, pretty on the windowpane, snow makes the world look completely different. That huge white blanket rolling over hills, the dirty slush in the gutters, cars piled high with white snow and cats plunging dismayed into vast drifts make us all look again at everyday things we take for granted.

The first time children see snow they are likely to be wildly excited, and want to rush straight out and get a proper look at it. A winter's walk through the snow, properly wrapped up of course, is a great joy, so shed a few years and get out there with them.

Building with snow

Snowmen are the traditional landmarks in a winter landscape. Before heading out to build one, make sure everyone has really thick gloves or is wearing two pairs. Cold hands take all the pleasure out of playing with snow. Put an old hat or cap, a carrot, a couple of lumps of coal or dark pebbles and a pipe, if you have one, in your pocket.

Show the children that rolling a snowball is the best way to build up bulk for the snowman's body. Note how the texture of the snow changes as it is packed together – from soft and fluffy to hard and solid.

The interesting thing about rolling a snowball in a park is that it leaves great grassy tracks in the ground. Try and roll the snow in a particular path to make a maze you can use for a later game.

The snowman's head can be made in the same way as the body. Add the hat and make a face.

Snow ducks, snow vehicles, snow wells, and other more elaborate sculptures, are all good alternatives. In many ways snow is a better building material than sand.

Snow experiments

Take a kettle of just-boiled water outside. Keep it away from the children, but let them watch as you pour a steady stream on to the snow or sprinkle it around carefully. What kind of patterns does the water make in the snow?

Do the children realize snow is frozen water? Fill a glass bowl and take it indoors. Mark the level it reaches on the bowl. How long does the snow take to melt? Is the level of the melted snow the same as the snow itself?

Safety notes
Children may be tempted to walk on a pond covered in ice, so make sure they understand that this is dangerous, especially when the weather is constantly hovering just on freezing. Never let them on ice without an adult right by them.

Snowflakes

When the temperature is really very cold, snowflakes are larger and more distinctly shaped and patterned. If you have a magnifying glass, use it to look at snowflakes on friends' coats or on the windowpane. The children will be surprised at the intricate symmetrical patterns they see.

Hail

Go outside in a hailstorm and let the children feel the hard drops of ice fall on their hands. Collect some in a large bowl for inspection.

Ice

On a freezing night put out several different-shaped containers full of water. In the morning the top layer will have frozen. You may be able to dig the ice out in complete sheets and compare the shapes. Let the children break the ice and see how thick it is.

Go to the pond and watch the ducks waddle over the ice. Even though it looks solid it is not wise to walk on it unless you live in an area where the winters are consistently very cold for several weeks at a time.

See Fun with water (pages 88-9) for more ideas on playing with ice.

Looking for bird prints, making snowmen, sledging – a snow-covered area of countryside is a real adventure playground.

Birds and birdwatching

Taking care of birds is not only enjoyable, it can be essential for their survival. In late autumn, winter and early spring, if there are prolonged frosts or heavy snowfalls, birds depend on us to supplement their diet. At these times they are more than willing to hop on to a convenient windowsill or gather in the garden for a daily feed. Children soon learn to recognize and identify their favourites.

Once the birds are used to your garden, they can be encouraged to nest and lay their eggs there. Providing a suitable nesting box will involve you in some hammering and sawing, but you'll find your patience more than adequately repaid.

Making a chart
Make a simple picture chart of the birds that visit your garden. Use a bird book to identify them. You can either cut pictures of the birds out of magazines, or help the children to draw them, along with the food each bird likes to eat.

Feeding
Putting out titbits regularly throughout the year is the way to make firm feathered friends. Birds appreciate bacon rind or other fat, stale bread (soak this in water or milk), small pieces of cooked meat, unsalted nuts, dried fruit, coconut, bits of cheese and apple cores. The children can mix all the ingredients into a 'pudding', put it all in a mesh bag and hang it from a window frame, tree or washing line. In very cold or icy weather, the birds will also appreciate water. Check regularly that it has not frozen over.

Various types of bird seed, as well as peanuts in a mesh bag, are sold by pet shops.

Birdwatching
If you can get to the countryside easily, try a short birdwatching trip, preferably with a pair of small-sized binoculars and a good bird book. Explain why everyone has to walk quietly, dress unobtrusively and speak softly.

Encouraging a love of birds and other animal life will sharpen your children's sensibilities and encourage some understanding of conservation and other environmental issues.

Safety notes
An adult will have to saw up the wood for the nesting box. Place food out of reach of cats: even the most lethargic can spring unexpectedly to life at the sight of a bird pecking food off the lawn.

Home-made bird tables come in all shapes and sizes. A cover helps to keep the food dry.

A bird table

You can make a simple table out of a pole and a square of wood – the smaller the surface and the higher the table, the better from the point of view of keeping it safe from cats. Alternatively, if you only have a window ledge, hang a square or oblong piece of wood, big enough to take food and a bowl of water, from a conveniently placed hook and watch the birds gather by your window every morning. Take care that you or the children don't frighten them off.

Which birds come most often? Which are greedy and carry off the food? Which peck delicately or get pushed out of the way? Which like the seed mixture and which prefer foraging for insects?

A NESTING BOX

Birds can be infuriatingly unappreciative of your immaculate pet-shop nesting box, rejecting it in favour of an old flowerpot or hollow log, so don't spend money buying one. Make one with a saw, six pieces of wood, a couple of hinges and screws, or try disguising a flowerpot with straw and twigs and hanging this on the wall of your house near the window and bird table, or the south side of a tree (the south side offers more protection: northern side if you live in the southern hemisphere). Make sure the entrance to the nesting box is not too big so that you attract smaller birds like tits rather than the more aggressive starlings.

The children might like to hang some nesting material (twigs, wool, bits of material) from hooks near the nesting box or on your windowsill and see which the birds like best.

If the birds lay eggs, remember to tell the children not to touch them or they will be rejected by the parent birds.

At the theatre

Dramatic art takes various forms: plays, entertainments, ballets and other dance routines and mime all come under this heading. Regular visits to good quality shows suitable for children will help foster a love of plays and music which could last them all their lives. As with other trips out (see pages 74-5), very young children do need to be prepared for what they see if they are to get the most from it.

Of course you don't want to overwhelm the children with culture at this early age, but it's surprising just how much they can get out of public performances. Some they'll remember in great detail and will refer to out of the blue for years afterwards.

There's no business like show business... Checking the billboards (right) *and booking tickets are part of the fun.*

Children's shows

During school holidays theatres often put on children's shows. Some of these are very good quality, others not so good. Find out in advance the age range of the entertainment on offer, and ask around about the type of show it is. It's important that it is not geared for children younger or older than your own, or they will be bored and disappointed.

Really good children's entertainers are few and far between. It is best to avoid the mediocre and not be tempted to take a crowd of children just because it is the only entertainment available.

If your children do not like joining in or being hauled up on to the stage, do not sit in the front row where they are likely to be picked on and embarrassed. And do not force them to go up on the stage if it's not a popular idea. If they are not bouncing up and down and joining in the songs, actions and music, don't worry. Some children are so entranced by the spectacle that just absorbing it is quite enough excitement. Not all children respond in the same way to such shows.

Pantomimes

Popular in the UK, in recent years many of these have got out of hand and are so far from the original story as to be unrecognizable and confusing, not to mention appallingly vulgar and geared to an uncritical adult audience. Some though, are absolutely magical, so ask someone who's been or look carefully at reviews before booking.

Similarly, puppet shows, ice shows and magic shows can all be wonderful outings for children.

Ballet

Ballet classes for two-, three- and four-year-olds are quite common, though they seem to attract more girls than boys. Even the briefest grounding is good preparation for a visit to a real ballet company.

If you are going to visit a ballet, choose a series of very short ones and be prepared to come out at the interval. Sit near the front so that the stage doesn't look like a television set. Some children have become so used to watching them on the television that they have difficulty in imagining *real* people performing.

Mime

Mime is something children identify with. They can do it too. It doesn't involve verbal ability, or complicated dance steps.

Before going to a mime show, practise a little at home. Find out what sort of mime is likely to be showing. How would your children act that out? You'll have something to talk about during the show and when you come out, and it could spark off other mime ideas.

Concerts

Classical concerts are usually too long for pre-school children, though parts of a programme may be suitable. Again, it does mean being prepared to enter or leave at the interval. Try to visit special children's musical programmes, if possible, where children are encouraged to join in by singing along or clapping, and so on.

Throwing a party

Before the age of about three, a 'party' consists mainly of you presiding over tea trying to persuade the children to eat at least one healthy sandwich before launching into the cakes and ice-cream, and playing some simple games like 'Ring a ring o' roses'.

As the children get older, these events become more sophisticated – but even harder work if you are not careful. However, there are ways to make it easier on yourself and the guests, while ensuring that everyone still has a great time.

A word of warning: keep the lead-up to the party low-key, send your child to bed early the night before and try to keep the excitement level down. If he or she gets overwrought on the day, it could end in tears.

Numbers

Unless you're very experienced in these matters, don't invite the entire playgroup or nursery school class, but have no more than half a dozen children. It's also quieter and easier to keep an eye on every child to see he or she is having a good time and not getting left out; with too many children there the party can get out of hand and then no one enjoys themselves. Also, try to avoid inviting a high proportion of accident-prone children who are likely to break the birthday presents before your child has played with them.

Organization

One and a half hours is ample for three-year-olds, and two hours enough for anyone. Indicate the finishing time on the invitations so that parents who cannot stay know when to pick up their offspring. Have one or two low-key games when the children come in to acclimatize the quiet ones. New children arriving can join the game. After tea another quiet time will avoid the possibility of indigestion. If you own a video recorder, a cartoon show is a possibility, or put on a short puppet show yourself (see pages 24-5). Noisier games are best at the end of the party when everyone is warmed up.

Don't forget to take advantage of the weather. A game of football or hopscotch in the park, or a dip in a paddling pool, becomes an exciting occasion when all your friends are there.

Invite a parent with each child – they'll not all be able to come, but you will get a few helpers.

PARTY GAMES

Try to have plenty of games planned. You never know what your party will want to play, and it's wise to have several in reserve.

For **Shipwreck**, spread a few cushions around the room to represent rocks. Then put on some music. The children have to jump from rock to rock without falling in the water. If anyone is 'swimming' when the music stops they are shipwrecked and are out.

Sardines involves one child going off to hide and the others going to look for him or her. When the child is discovered the 'finder' climbs into the cupboard or under the bed too. The next child finding this pair joins them, and so on, until they are all squeezed into the same hiding place, making a tin of sardines.

Pass the orange is difficult for young children, but four- and five-year-olds enjoy it. The object is to pass an orange, or a tennis ball, by taking it from under one child's chin with your own chin and passing it round the group. No hands!

The usual games of 'Musical bumps', 'The farmer's in his den' and 'Follow my leader' are all good standbys. Be ready to adapt to a quiet or noisy game depending on the state of mind of your guests! Try not to over-react if one child gets upset. If everyone seems bent on getting tired and emotional, fall back on 'Dead fishes'. Everyone lies on the floor and stays absolutely still. If you move, you're out!

Food

Keep this attractive but simple. Open sandwiches are best, otherwise the bread will be carefully peeled off and left on the table. Or make a striped sandwich loaf (see page 85) using two or three favourite fillings such as cream cheese, peanut butter and jam (jelly). Rolled sandwiches are also popular. Spread thin slices of bread with a filling, cut off the crusts and roll up tightly. Cut to make little sandwiches that look like Swiss rolls.

Apart from sandwiches and some cheesy savouries, all you need are a few chocolate biscuits (cookies), some ice-cream and a not-too-rich cake. (All children love blowing out the candles on a birthday cake!) The ice-cream is best served as character cornets (cones). Use chocolate drops (M & Ms) for eyes, a cherry for a nose and angelica for the mouth. The cone becomes a jester's hat.

After the party

Take-home presents of balloons, stickers, a few grapes, a wrapped sweet or two (some candy) and simple toys, given away in a 'booty bag' have become rather the norm. Children love them and will have come to expect them from other parties.

It may mean an afternoon's hard work, but a party will be a very special occasion for your child.

Mother's Day

Mother's Day has a long tradition and provides a perfect excuse for children to show off their card- and gift-making skills as well as express their appreciation of a difficult job! Fathers or older children will need to be brought in to help with these preparations, so this section is directed at them.

Breakfast in bed

Older pre-school children will enjoy taking their mother breakfast in bed. A tray containing a paper napkin, small vase of flowers, a little present and card, and eggs, orange juice and toast to eat, will be a real treat to a hard-working mum. Instead of a vase of flowers, try floating a few flower heads in a little glass dish.

Downstairs welcome

Cut out large triangles from pieces of coloured craft (construction) paper. Small helpers can decorate the edges of the triangles with a pattern, or perhaps sequins or glitter (see below). Coloured glitter is very effective.

On each one write a letter to make up a short message to mother – 'Hello Mum' or 'Happy Mother's Day' or whatever seems appropriate. Some children might manage this themselves. Other triangles can be coloured in with a pattern to provide the gaps between words. Help the children to attach the message with sticky tape to a long piece of ribbon and hang this like bunting across a downstairs room, or across a doorway as a greeting to mother.

Special cards

Young children could try drawing themselves as a baby to remind mother of what it's all about!

Pressed flowers (see pages 86-7) – mother's favourite – glued lightly to a piece of card look very pretty.

Children, perhaps with assistance from an older child or dad, trace out the letters of the word 'mum' or 'mother' on the front of a horizontally folded piece of card and apply a thin layer of glue along the lines. Sequins can then be stuck on to the glue. A little more glue dabbed on around the card will provide a base for some glitter. Shake off excess carefully.

MOTHER'S DAY DOLL
You'll need:
washing-up mop (dish mop)
a wooden spoon
long pipe cleaners
piece of material long enough to cover the spoon
yoghurt pot
clear sticky tape

Younger children, with a little help, can manage most of the stages in making 'Mother'.

1 Bind together the mop and spoon to make a face framed with a halo of rather messy hair. Use sticky tape top and bottom to make sure they don't move.

2 Make a hole in the middle of your material and push it up from the bottom; attach with string or wool at the 'neck'.

3 Stick the ends of the spoon and mop into a hole made in the yoghurt pot. Bind this with sticky tape too. Join a couple of pipe cleaners together, turn over the ends to make hands. Wrap around the spoon and mop near the top, under the material. Cut holes in the material and poke the 'arms' through.

4 Paint the spoon 'face' or use felt tips.

5 Hang a little bag from one arm, or fold the arms in and rest a tiny baby doll in the crook.

Mother's Day collage

Look out favourite photographs of members of the family, postcards of places you've been together, bits and pieces that will have a meaning to mother such as a special drawing by a young child, or a piece of material from baby's first item of clothing, and help the children cut out and stick these things together on a big piece of card labelled 'Happy Mother's Day'.

Although one day a year is designated as Mother's Day, many of these ideas can be used at other times of the year. The children might like to take their mother breakfast in bed on her birthday, for example, and home-made birthday cards make the occasion more special.

A collage or other gift is a good way for a child to show his or her appreciation at any time.

Mother's Day gives the rest of the family a chance to hatch an appreciative breakfast plot.

Hallowe'en

Hallowe'en is a pretty spooky occasion and has a long association with witchcraft, black magic and the occult. But it is also an excellent opportunity to dress up, frighten unsuspecting adults, play 'Trick or treat' and throw a party.

Dressing up

Always keep an old clothes' box around, so that the children can experiment at all times of the year and get into the swing of 'being someone else'.

Some ideas for spooky personae include:

A *mummy* involves finding a small helper and wrapping a *willing* child up from head to toe in bandages. Apply vegetable dye or paint to look like mould and dried blood, draw black circles round the eyes and mouth and you'll have a ghoul fit to terrify anyone.

A *witch* will need a cloak made out of black lining material with a drawstring around the neck, with a black leotard and tights – or any dark clothes underneath. Make a very simple hat and stick raffia, wool or crêpe paper strands around the inside of the rim to look like horrible hair. Hang a toy spider (or a tomato stalk) from one ear, make a broomstick from a broom handle and twigs, apply ghoulish make-up, and wait for the 'Oohs' and 'Aaahs'.

A *black cat* is a popular character to model. A black leotard, an old black velvet jacket (use the sleeves to make the cat's 'arms'), black tights, furry ears on a headband, and a furry tail stiffened with wire, make a good, cheap costume.

A *ghost* is a very easy costume. Cut eye holes in a big, old sheet, and draw round them in black charcoal or felt tip, then cut out a sad, droopy mouth and draw round that. Now set your phantom to frighten the guests.

Decorating the room

Spider's webs can be made from a piece of black drawing paper: help the children to fold and cut it to make the correct shape. Tomato stalks make realistic-looking spiders, so attach these with pieces of thread to the webs and hang them on the walls and in corners.

Safety notes
An adult will need to hollow out the vegetables and make incisions for the faces, but take advice from the children on what kind of expression the faces should show.

Some of these ideas could frighten the very young, so make sure tiny brothers and sisters are out of the way and look after the nervous.

LANTERNS
Hollow out the vegetables (pumpkins are favourites), cut faces with different expressions in them, and stand wax night-lights inside. These can be lit and hung from hooks or stood on mantelshelves – very spooky in an otherwise dark room. Make sure they cannot be knocked over, or even better keep them out of doors.

Bats can be cut out from more black paper and hung from doorways. Shine lights so that their shadows appears larger than life.

Ghoulish fingers are made from lengths of string dipped in water. Hang these from the ceiling so that they brush the heads of the children.

Games

Apple bobbing is a traditional game. Choose tiny apples, or the children won't have a chance of getting them! Float the apples in a bucket of water and see who can capture the most with their mouths. They'll get very wet, so be prepared with aprons and a groundsheet.

   If you can't face the mess made by bobbing, hang apples on strings (push string through the middle with a darning needle and tie a knot the other end) at about child head height. Remember, no hands!

Pin the spider on the web is another Hallowe'en game. Attach one of the spider's webs to a piece of card, mark a place where the spider should be, then blindfold each child in turn and let him or her fix the 'spider' to the web. The child whose spider is nearest the mark wins.

This is not as easy as it looks – younger children will have to be 'helped' to catch their apples!

Spring festivals

Easter, the Muslim festival Eid to mark the end of Ramadan, the Jewish Passover and the Hindu festival Holi, are all jolly times for children, and provide good occasions for dressing up, telling stories and dancing as well as the opportunity to talk about the ways people from many cultures celebrate their religious festivals. These activities are best for a group of children from different backgrounds.

Eid

Muslims celebrate Eid with prayers *(Namaz)* at home or at their mosque. They usually have new clothes to wear and the children receive *'Eidy'* – presents or money. They cook sweets (candies), decorate eggs (see right) and visit friends and relations.

'Eid Mubarak' means 'Happy Eid', and can be written in Arabic script on a poster and decorated. This message can also be used on cards to give to friends and relations, or perhaps the children might prefer to draw and colour in a picture of a mosque.

Some floaty materials in the dressing-up box are also a good idea – they can be used to provide saris or duppatas (the shawl that goes across the shoulders or over the head).

Holi

Holi is celebrated by offering food – almonds, groundnuts and fruit, for instance – to God in the temples. The coconut is a symbol of fertility in Hinduism and so very appropriate in a spring festival when everything is fresh and growing.

In India, Holi processions take place out of doors. The people wear old clothes and throw brightly coloured powder or paint at each other, squirt water pistols, and generally indulge in all kinds of mischief – it is a perfect festival for children! At night coconuts are roasted on bonfires. It's messy, but if the children wear really old clothes, throwing paint or confetti at each other is good fun.

Holi originates in the childhood of the Lord Krishna, incarnation of the god Vishnu. Stories about Krishna abound and it is worth seeking out some simpler ones in the library to read at story time.

Dressing up is also a colourful way to celebrate Holi. Use scarves for veils and saris, and give the children bells to ring and drums to play to some authentic Indian music.

DECORATED EGGS

Use hard-boiled eggs rather than raw ones with the middles blown out, as they're easier for children to handle. When they are cold they can be painted with felt tips or thick powder paint in bright designs. 'Hair' (bits of wool) and 'beards' (cottonwool) stick well.

Another good idea is to draw on raw eggs with a small birthday candle. Older children can write initials, but designs are very effective. Then place the eggs in cold water to which you've added a touch of food colouring. Hard boil the eggs for about 10 minutes. The waxed bits will not absorb the dye and will stand out against a coloured background.

Passover

Passover is the Jewish spring festival which lasts for eight days and is in memory of the Jews escaping from slavery in Egypt. On the first night there is a special feast called the Seder feast, which is very much a family affair (see page 114). At the feast the youngest member of the family asks four traditional questions, the answers to which tell the story of Haggadah: the freeing of Israel, home of the Jews.

Why not tell the Bible story of the plagues of Egypt and the escape of the Jews across the Red Sea? The children might like to act it out. Candles around the room would be festive and appropriate.

Easter

Just as Eid comes at the end of the Muslim fast, Ramadan, so in the Christian calendar Easter marks the end of Lent and the Resurrection of Christ. It is also a festival of spring 'renewal', which is why the symbols of new-born baby chicks and rabbits came to be associated with Easter.

Cards for friends and relations are easy to make. Help the children cut out rabbit and chick-shaped cards and colour them in. Alternatively, provide some coloured paper and suggest that the children cut out half-egg shapes with jagged edges to look as if they've cracked. On another piece of paper they can draw chicks, or make them out of fluffy yellow cottonwool (absorbent cotton) or hamster bedding. Stick the egg shapes above and below the chicks and cut round to make attractive cards.

Brightly painted eggs provide pretty ornaments all the year round, not just at Easter.

Winter festivals

Whether your family or playgroup celebrates Christmas, or Diwali, or the Chinese New Year, fairy lights, tinsel, glitter, prayers, happy families, presents, parties and favourite foods are all part and parcel of the celebrations. Preparing for festivals is great fun and can teach children a good deal about cultures other than their own.

Christmas

The build-up to Christmas is so long these days that helping to decorate the home or playgroup and thinking about presents they can give (rather than the ones they'll receive!) is a good distraction for children.

Advent starts on 1 December and goes on until Christmas Eve. In the religious calendar, it is traditionally a period of self-denial. Many Advent calendars have a religious content, others simply represent seasonal activities or symbols such as stars and snowmen.

An Advent box calendar is a good gift for you or an older child to make for a small child. You'll need 24 small boxes (herb boxes, for example). Each should be painted a jolly colour with thick powder paint, with a picture and number (1 to 24 inclusive) added in another colour. Stick the boxes to a large piece of card and hang it on the wall. Inside each one hide a few nuts and raisins, a tiny toy, small crayons or a little Christmas poem. Or put in the figures and animals that make up the Christmas crib. Each day the child can open a box and find a gift.

Stencilled Christmas cards are very professional looking. Choose simple designs – a stylized tree, a star, candle, robin, snowman – and suggest the children draw the outlines on to a card. These are then cut out and laid on white, folded, watercolour paper. Hold the stencil in position while the children paint on watercolour. If they intend to use more than one colour, remember to let the first layer dry.

Silhouette cards can be made out of coloured thick card and shapes of thinnish black paper. (To avoid sticky finger collage, help the children apply glue to the shapes by turning them upside-down on some lining paper or newsprint and pasting them before going anywhere near the card.) Press the shapes lightly into place and smooth with a clean cloth.

Gifts which the children can make for friends and relations include pomanders (oranges stuffed with cloves), bookmarks and herb bags.

Safety notes
Scissors are a big feature in these activities, and some involve sparklers. Careful supervision is essential.

Acting out the nativity story reminds children of the true meaning of Christmas.

Diwali

Diwali, in slightly different variations, is celebrated by Hindus, Sikhs and Jains and is one of the world's oldest religious festivals. Like Christmas, at Diwali families and friends spend time together and exchange gifts and cards. The festival falls each year around the end of October or beginning of November and lasts for five days.

Diwali originates in the story of Rama and his wife Sita. Sita was abducted by the demon Ravan and rescued with the help of Hanuman, the Monkey God. Diwali celebrates the reunion of Rama and Sita.

On the first day of Diwali, houses and shops are scrubbed clean and doorsteps decorated with multi-coloured rangoli designs. These can be drawn on paper using chalk and charcoal. Powder paint or coloured sand can then be sprinkled inside a drawn outline.

Tinsel, glitter, brightly coloured aluminium foil, Diwa lamps and rangoli patterns can all be combined to make Diwali cards – the brighter and shinier the better. Fireworks and crackers are usually part of the celebrations on the second day of the festival. It's probably best to limit these to sparklers for young children.

On the third day of Diwali, the Diwa lamps are lit. These are simple little clay dishes, and can be made very easily from ready-made clay. Tightly rolled cottonwool (absorbent cotton) soaked in vegetable oil and coiled inside the lamp makes the wicks.

Food and flowers are exchanged on the fourth day. The children could make flower garlands out of real flowers (if there are any left in the garden) or tissue paper threaded on to wool or cotton thread.

On the final day, people give each other sweets (candies).

Hand painting is an excellent way to celebrate Diwali, and fun for children of all cultures.

Hanuka

This Jewish festival takes place in December each year and celebrates the miraculous lighting of candles in the temple of Jerusalem by Judas Maccabeus. Although there was only enough oil left to keep the menorah alight for one day, it lasted eight. Hanuka lasts eight days, and in Jewish homes one candle is lit on each day of the festival, so that by the eighth day, there are eight candles alight.

Hanuka is party time, so a children's party with lots of candles and small home-made gifts is an excellent way to celebrate.

Yuan Tan (Chinese New Year)

The date of Yuan Tan is determined by the Chinese calendar; it falls somewhere between the middle of January and the middle of February. On this day, all Chinese people become one year older.

If you live in a city with a large Chinese population, like London or San Francisco, you will be able to see a New Year procession, complete with dragons, colourful masks, clashing cymbals and firecrackers. In China, dragons are symbols of happiness and good luck and frighten away any evil spirits left behind by the old year.

Red is the colour of happiness and good luck. Red paper cut-outs are pasted on the windows to give the room some colour, and money is wrapped in red paper and given to children. Oranges are traditional good luck presents.

Help the children make a banner to hang across the room. Write on it 'Gung Ho Sun Hse' (Happy New Year) for the children to colour in or paint; they might also like to paint on some red geometric shapes or colourful dragons.

Cut out red paper shapes, and make some lanterns to hang at the window. Alternatively, try painting some clay models with shiny red 'sugar' paint (powder paint mixed with some sugar).

In San Francisco, the Chinese community makes a 38 m (125 ft) long dragon of golden silk and velvet; you could suggest that the children make a human dragon. Each child decorates a cardboard box with paint, red streamers to represent fire, strips of aluminium foil, foil bottle or carton tops, and then wears it with his or her head sticking out the top. The dragon is made by each child holding the waist of the child in front.

Another idea is for the first child to wear a box on his or her head, with eyeholes cut out. A colourful blanket or two over the other children make a jolly, rather wobbly, alternative dragon.

Colourful dragons roam the streets as part of the Chinese New Year celebrations.

Festival cooking

During those frustrating days before a holiday or festival, when everyone is bursting with anticipation, and you're stuck in the kitchen preparing endless meals, children need diverting. Making special sweets, pastries and other goodies for the feasts mentioned in this book is ideal. (Most of these goodies contain a fair amount of sugar, so should be considered occasional treats and not everyday snacks.)

Whichever festival you are celebrating, most of these culinary goodies can be wrapped in tissue paper and given away as presents.

Passover and Rosh Hashana (Jewish New Year)

At Passover a traditional meal of lamb, roasted eggs, apples, nuts, bitter herbs and watercress is served on special Seder dishes, with unleavened bread. You could include some of these ingredients in a feast; one of the children might have a Seder dish to show the group.

At Rosh Hashana it is the custom to eat an apple dipped in honey to show that the New Year will be fruitful. This is a fairly simple treat for you and the children to prepare; alternatively, try making a honey cake.

Easter

Help the children to make some marzipan (see right) and cut out chicks and rabbits for cake decorations. If you are baking hot cross buns, the more dextrous children can pipe the paste cross on to the buns just before baking, and gloss the finished products when they come out of the oven with a mixture of castor sugar and milk melted together.

Christmas

Frosted fruit is easy to prepare. Take some red apples, black grapes and green pears, an egg white and some castor sugar. Get one or two children to polish the apples and pears until they are gleaming nicely, while you or another child whisks up the egg white lightly. Pour the sugar on to a piece of aluminium foil or a dinner plate.

One child can dip a paintbrush in the egg white and paint it in streaks on the fruit. Another can then roll each piece of fruit carefully in the sugar. Keep the grapes in a bunch and just dab each one with egg white. A child can dip the bunch in the sugar and shake off the excess.

Pile the fruit in a dish along with pine cones, oranges and, perhaps, a few Christmas decorations.

HONEY CAKE

You'll need:
250 g (8 oz./2 cups) honey
2 eggs
½ tsp bicarbonate of soda
5 fl. oz. (¼ pt) warm water
125 g (4 oz./1 cup) sugar
375 g (12 oz./3 cups) self-raising (all-purpose) flour
1 tsp ginger
3 tsp oil
½ tsp all spice
almonds

1 Sieve the flour, ginger, bicarbonate of soda, and spice together.
2 Warm the honey.
3 Beat the eggs and sugar until they are frothy, then add the oil and honey.
4 Add the rest of the dry ingredients alternately with the water. Mix until you have a thin batter.
5 Sprinkle a 22.5 cm (9 in.) tin with almonds, pour in the batter, and bake for an hour at 375°F (Gas Mark 4).

MAKING SEVIANYA

Sevianya is the traditional sweet or pudding served at Eid. Children can help at various stages in the preparation and making.

1 Boil down 1 litre (2 pints) of milk until it has reduced by half and thickened. Add sugar to taste and two cardamom pods.
2 When the mixture is creamy, add some vermicelli and simmer until the vermicelli is soft and the pudding thick and creamy. Remove the cardamom pods. Serve warm or chilled.
3 Pistachio nuts can be sprinkled on top before serving (but remember young children can choke on whole nuts), or sprinkle the pudding with cinnamon.

Yuan Tan (Chinese New Year)

To encourage the kitchen god to give a good report to heaven about the state of their kitchens, the Chinese would prepare a feast for him, consisting of sweets, pastries and fruit, and set it out on a table with red candles and incense.

Let the children lay out the table with some of these offerings and help them to make Jiaozi. These are sweet dumplings made by mixing white flour, nuts and sugar with water. A small coin is traditionally rolled into the centre of each one, but if you choose to do this, make sure the children are aware of the dangers.

Holi

Coconut is a traditional Holi food. It is supposed to be roasted, but if you find this a bit daunting, simply use the milk to make drinks and cut up the flesh to share it out.

Safety notes

During all cooking activities, be very watchful of saucepan handles sticking out, sharp knives left on low surfaces and oven doors left open – all are potential hazards for the under-fives.

MARZIPAN DATES

For about two dozen, you'll need:
1 box dates
100 g (4 oz./1 cup) ground almonds
almond essence
1 egg
50 g (2 oz./½ cup) castor sugar
50 g (2 oz./½ cup) icing sugar (or 1 cup confectioner's sugar)
food colouring (optional)

1 Stone the dates (you should do this for the children).
2 Meantime, one child can sift the icing sugar into a basin and add the castor sugar and ground almonds. Another can be mixing up two tablespoons of lightly beaten egg with a few drops of almond essence.
3 This should be stirred into the sugar mixture and mixed to a firm dough.
4 Sprinkle a work surface with castor sugar and knead the dough to make marzipan.
5 If you are using food colouring (and don't forget it does contain additives), divide the marzipan in half and add one colour to one lot, another to the other lot. Knead again, but not too much or the mixture will spoil.
6 Helpers can stuff each date with a stone-shaped piece of marzipan and roll it in castor sugar.

Cooking for a special day – and an opportunity for some team work.

Booklist

Baker, Carol, *Carol Baker's Fun to Learn Playpack* (Macdonald)
Baker, Carol *Reading Through Play: The Easy Way to Teach Your Child* (Macdonald)
Barton *Storytelling and Reading Aloud at Home, at School and in the Community* (Heinemann)
Berg, Leila *Reading and Learning* (Routledge and Kegan Paul)
Cobb, Vicki *Bet You Can't* (Harper and Row)
Cobb, Vicki *Hardware Store Science Experiments* (Harper and Row)
Cobb, Vicki *Science Experiments You Can Eat* (Harper and Row)
Crowe, Brenda *Play Is a Feeling* (Allen & Unwin)
Gregg, E. *What to Do When There's Nothing to Do* (Penguin)
Herbert, Don *Mr Wizard's Experiments for Young Scientists* (Doubleday)
Herbert, Don *Mr Wizard's Supermarket Science* (Random House)
Jameson, K. *Pre-School and Infant Art* (Studio Vista)
Katz, Adrienne *A World in Your Kitchen* (Piatkus)
Katz, Adrienne *Naturewatch* (Piatkus)
Newson, J. and E. *Toys and Playthings* (Penguin)
November, Janet *Story of a Home Playgroup* (Allen & Unwin)
Taylor and Strickland *Family Storybook Reading* (Heinemann)
Yardley, Alice *Preparing Your Child for School* (Franklin Watts)

Useful addresses

Pre-School Playgroups Association (PPA)
Alford House
Aveline Street
London SE11 5DH
(in USA – PCPI, PO Box 31335, Phoenix, Arizona 85046)

British Standards Institution
Consumer Affairs Department
2 Park Street
London W1A 2BS
(for a leaflet on safety regulations for toys and equipment)

National Children's Bureau
7 Wakely Street
London EC14 7QF
(activities and resources for parents of handicapped children)

The National Trust
PO Box 30
Beckenham
Kent
BR3 4TL

The Woodland Trust
Autumn Park
Dysart Road
Grantham
Lincolnshire
NG31 6LL

Catalogues by post

James Galt Toys Ltd
Brookfield Road
Cheadle
Cheshire
(catalogue of toys)

Offspring
E.J. Arnold and Son Ltd
Butterley Street
Leeds
Yorkshire
LS10 3TS

Early Learning Centre
Hawksworth
Swindon
Wiltshire
SN2 1TT

Community Playthings
Darvell
Robertsbridge
East Sussex
TN32 5DR

Acknowledgements

Swallow Publishing Limited wish to thank the following organizations and individuals for their help in the production of *Pre-School Play Activities*. We apologize to anyone we may have omitted to mention.

Playgroups/Nursery schools
The staff and children of:
Greygates Nursery, London N10
Henry Cavendish Primary School, London SW12
Hornsey Rise Nursery, London N8
St Erkenwald playgroup, Barking, Essex

Photographs
David Allen 37, 57, 71, 103; Art Directors 63, 109, 111; John Campbell cover, title, 8, 9, 10, 11, 13, 14, 15, 17, 19, 20/21, 22, 23, 25, 27, 28, 29, 30, 32, 35, 38, 41, 43, 45, 46, 48/49, 49, 51, 53, 55, 57, 59, 67, 68, 73, 75, 77, 79, 82/83, 84/85, 86, 88/89, 89, 93, 95, 99, 100, 101, 105, 107, 113; Format 112; Sally and Richard Greenhill 90/91; Susan Griggs 64, 96; Elaine Partington 97; Piatkus Books 62/63; Vision International 39, 81, 103, 115; Zefa 60, 61, 74

Note: Numbers in italic refer to illustrations

action rhymes 46, 55; *46*
action words 57
Advent calendar 110
airport 74
Alan Alert 27; *27*
algae 76
animals 80-1
  – tracks 69; *68*
  – wild 69
  see also birds, pets
ant colony 94
apple bobbing 107; *107*
art gallery 75
articulated doll 26

ball games 62, 63
ballet 101
balloon 67
bank 71
bats 107; *107*
beach 90-1; *90-1*
bedroom blackboard 12, 57; *57*
birds 73, 98-9
  – feeding 98; *99*
  – prints 69; *97*
  – table 99; *99*
  – watching 98
black cat 106
blackberrying *73*
books 54-5
bottle octave 47; *47*
breakfast in bed 104
bubble bowl 88
bulbs 78

canals 75
card pairs 31; *30*
cards
  – Christmas 110
  – Easter 109
  – Eid 108
  – Mother's Day 104
  – silhouette 110
chalks 12, 57; *57*
charts
  – bird 98
  – colour 55

  – growing 79
  – growth 82
  – money 42
  – number 31; *31*
  – picture 33
  – weighing teddy 33; *33*
Chinese New Year *see* Yuan Tan
children's shows 101
  see also theatre
Christmas 110; *111*
  – cooking 114
clay 40
clock face 20; *20-1*
collage 18-19; *9, 19*
  – fabric 18
  – Mother's Day 105
  – nature 19
  – paper 18
  – paper sculpture 18
  – pressed flower 87
  – rainy day 65
  – snow *9*
  – windy day 66
collecting 28-9
  – using collections 29
colour 13, 15
  – chart 55
  – wheel 27
combine harvester 81
comparisons 29
concerts 101
conservation 73, 77, 98
cooking 33, 39, 114-15; *39, 115*
  – games 23, 92
crayons 12; *13*
crops 81

dancing 47, 48
Diwali 112; *112*
doll's scarves 50
dominoes 31
dragonflies 77
drawing 12-13; *13*
dressing up 22-3, 106, 108; *22, 23*

Easter 109, 114; *109*
eggs, decorated 108; *109*
Eid 108, 114
electricity 39
environmental print 71
exercises 48; *48-9*

fantasy games 22-3
farm 80-1; *81*
  – games 81
fiddling board 37; *37*
fire station 75; *75*
fishing 76; *77*
  – games 39; *38*

floating 89
flowers
  – drying 87
  – parts of *87*
  – pressing 87; *8, 86*
  – wild 86-7
food
  – for parties 103
  – for picnics 84-5
footprints 16; *17*
  – animal 69
  – bird *97*
frogs 77
frosted fruit 114

garden toys 61; *61*
ghost 106
glove puppet theatre 24; *24, 25*

Hallowe'en 106-7
handprints 15, 16; *17*
handstands 48; *8*
Hanuka 112
harbour 75
herb windowbox 79
Holi 108
  – cooking 115
honey cake 114

ice 97
  – cubes 88
Jewish New Year *see* Rosh Hashana
jigsaw puzzles 52-3; *53*
  – commercial 53
  – three dimensional 52
  – word 52
jungle games 60

kite 67; *67*
knitting 50-1; *51*

labelling 56
lanterns 106; *106*
leaves 72
library 56

machinery 37
  – farm 81
magnets 39; *38*
making faces 49
marbling 17
marzipan dates 115
measuring 32-3
  – irregular objects 33
mess 8, 13, 112
mechanics board 37; *37*
memory games 34-5
mime 101
mobiles 26

modelling 40-1; *11, 41*
money 42
  – chart 42
  – pocket 43
  – sorting 42
mosaics 18
Mother's day 104-5; *105*
  – doll 104; *104*
mummy 106
museum 75
music 46-7
musical instruments 47
'My grandmother went to market' 34

neapolitan sandwiches 85; *85*
nesting box 99: *99*
newts 77
'The North Wind Doth Blow' 21
numbers 30-1
  – game 31

obstacle course 60
oil and water 88
outdoor games 62-3; *62-3*

paddling pool 60, 61
paint pad 16
paintbrushes 13
painting 12-13, 14-15; *9, 10, 13*
  – finger 15
  – models 41
pantomimes 101
paper dart 67
papier mâché 40
parachute 67; *67*
parts of the body 53
party 102-3; *103*
  – games 102
  – Hanuka 112
  – numbers 102
  – organization 102
Passover 109
  – cooking 114
paste 18
patchwork squares 50
pelmanism *see* card pairs
pencils 12
pets 58-9; *59*
picnic 84-5; *84-5*
picture books 55
picture calendar 21
picture charts 56
picture diary 75
picture/word snap 56
plants 82-3; *82-3*
  – *see also* seeds, bulbs
plaster cast 69; *11, 68*
Plasticine 40

playdough
  – making 40
  see also modelling
playhouse 23
playing house 23
playing shop 42-3; *43*
plumbing 39
pond skaters 76
ponds 76-7
ports 75
Post Office 70
potatoes 83; *83*
printing
  – block 16; *16*
  – letter 16; *16*
  – roller 16
puppets 24-5; *25*
  – glove 24; *8, 25*
  – sock 24
  – wooden spoon 24-5

races 63
rain 64-5; *64*
rainbows 65; *65*
reading 54-5, 56-7; *55*
rhymes 55
  – action 46, 55; *46*
river trips 75
road safety 70
rock pool 90
role play 42
rope games 62
Rosh Hashana
  – cooking 114
rubbings 19

safety 12, 18, 23, 26, 29, 36, 39, 45, 48, 51, 58, 60, 76, 80, 82, 88, 91, 92, 94, 96, 110, 115
sand 90, 92-3; *93*
  – bag dolls 92
  – casts 93
  – punch bags 93
sausage animals 51
scales 33; *32*
scribbling 12, 57; *57*
seasons 21
seaweed 91; *90-1*
seeds
  – of trees 72; *72*
  – planting 78-9; *79*
Sevianya 114
sewing 44
  – cards 44; *44*
  – gloves 44
shapes 55
shells 91; *91*
shoelaces 45; *45*
shopping 43

shops 70; *71*
  see also playing shop
sinking 89
Slippery Sid 26; *10, 27*
snow 96-7; *97*
  – building snowmen 96
  – experiments with 96
  – snowflakes 97
soil 78
somersaults 48
sorting 28-9; *26, 29*
sponges 14; *10, 14*
'Spring' 21
stencils 15
stick insects 94-5; *95*
story-acting 23
straws 15; *15*
sunflowers 78; *78*
swimming 48; *48*

tent adventures 60
theatre 100-1; *100, 101*
threading 44-5
time 20-1; *20-1*
toads 77
toilet roll toys 26; *10, 27*
toothbrush 15; *10, 14*
tractors 81
tray game 34; *35*
tree house 61
trees 72-3; *9, 73*
tug-of-war 63; *63*

wallcharts *see* charts
water-lilies 76
water measurers 76
water play 88-9; *88-9, 89*
wax 88
weaving 45
  – box *45*
  – straws 45
weighing 32-3; *32*
'What did we do today?' 34
'What was he wearing?' 35
wheels 36
whirligig beetles 76
'Who has seen the wind?' 66
wildlife 85
wind 66-7
witch 107
woodwork 36-7
worms 95
wrapping paper 17
writing 57

Yuan Tan 112-3; *113*
  – cooking 115

zoo 75; *74*